DATE DUE

DE 2 3 '13			
MAY 0 4 2015			
MAY 2 1 2015			
FEB 2 7 2019			

1st EDITION

Perspectives on Diseases and Disorders

Asperger Syndrome

Arthur Gillard

Book Editor

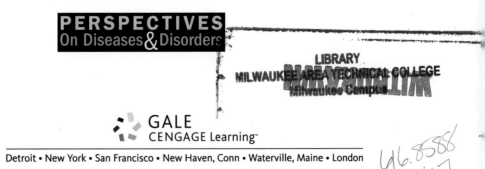

GALE
CENGAGE Learning

Detroit • New York • San Francisco • New Haven, Conn • Waterville, Maine • London

Christine Nasso, *Publisher*
Elizabeth Des Chenes, *Managing Editor*

For more information, contact:
Greenhaven Press
27500 Drake Rd.
Farmington Hills, MI 48331-3535
Or you can visit our Internet site at gale.cengage.com

For product information and technology assistance, contact us at

Gale Customer Support, 1-800-877-4253
For permission to use material from this text or product, submit all requests online at
www.cengage.com/permissions

Further permissions questions can be e-mailed to permissionrequest@cengage.com

Articles in Greenhaven Press anthologies are often edited for length to meet page requirements. In addition, original titles of these works are changed to clearly present the main thesis and to explicitly indicate the author's opinion. Every effort is made to ensure that Greenhaven Press accurately reflects the original intent of the authors. Every effort has been made to trace the owners of copyrighted material.

Cover image copyright © BSIP Phototake—All rights reserved.

LIBRARY OF CONGRESS CATALOGING-IN-PUBLICATION DATA

Asperger syndrome / Arthur Gillard, book editor.
    p. cm. -- (Perspectives on diseases and disorders)
  Summary: "Asperger Syndrome: Understanding Asperger Syndrome; Controversies About Asperger Syndrome; Personal Experiences with Asperger Syndrome"-- Provided by publisher.
  Includes bibliographical references and index.
  ISBN 978-0-7377-5771-2 (hardback)
  1. Asperger's syndrome--Popular works. I. Gillard, Arthur.
  RC553.A88A787 2011
  616.85'8832--dc22

                             2011006229

Printed in the United States of America
1 2 3 4 5 6 7 15 14 13 12 11

CONTENTS

Susan Ashley

Asperger syndrome is a pervasive developmental disorder characterized by problems such as repetitive routines, obsessive interest in a few topics, and problems with socializing.

Lisa. A. Ruble and Melissa Wheatley

Asperger syndrome has many similarities to autism and other pervasive developmental disorders. The *Diagnostic and Statistical Manual of Mental Disorders* defines how to diagnose and distinguish these conditions.

Tony Attwood

Depending on their circumstances and personality, children with Asperger syndrome will respond to their differences through escapist fantasy, imitating others, self-blame, or blaming others for their problems.

CHAPTER 2   Controversies About Asperger Syndrome

CHAPTER 3 Personal Experiences with
Asperger Syndrome

FOREWORD

"Medicine, to produce health, has to examine disease."
—Plutarch

Independent research on a health issue is often the first step to complement discussions with a physician. But locating accurate, well-organized, understandable medical information can be a challenge. A simple Internet search on terms such as "cancer" or "diabetes," for example, returns an intimidating number of results. Sifting through the results can be daunting, particularly when some of the information is inconsistent or even contradictory. The Greenhaven Press series Perspectives on Diseases and Disorders offers a solution to the often overwhelming nature of researching diseases and disorders.

From the clinical to the personal, titles in the Perspectives on Diseases and Disorders series provide students and other researchers with authoritative, accessible information in unique anthologies that include basic information about the disease or disorder, controversial aspects of diagnosis and treatment, and first-person accounts of those impacted by the disease. The result is a well-rounded combination of primary and secondary sources that, together, provide the reader with a better understanding of the disease or disorder.

Each volume in Perspectives on Diseases and Disorders explores a particular disease or disorder in detail. Material for each volume is carefully selected from a wide range of sources, including encyclopedias, journals, newspapers, non-fiction books, speeches, government documents, pamphlets, organization newsletters, and position papers. Articles in the first chapter provide an authoritative, up-to-date overview that covers symptoms, causes and effects, treatments, cures, and medical advances. The second chapter presents a substantial number of opposing viewpoints on controversial treatments and other current debates relating to the volume topic. The third chapter offers a variety of personal perspectives on the disease or disorder. Patients, doctors, caregivers, and loved ones represent just some of the voices found in this narrative chapter.

Each Perspectives on Diseases and Disorders volume also includes:

- An **annotated table of contents** that provides a brief summary of each article in the volume.
- An **introduction** specific to the volume topic.
- Full-color **charts and graphs** to illustrate key points, concepts, and theories.
- Full-color **photos** that show aspects of the disease or disorder and enhance textual material.
- **"Fast Facts"** that highlight pertinent additional statistics and surprising points.
- A **glossary** providing users with definitions of important terms.
- A **chronology** of important dates relating to the disease or disorder.
- An annotated list of **organizations to contact** for students and other readers seeking additional information.
- A **bibliography** of additional books and periodicals for further research.
- A detailed **subject index** that allows readers to quickly find the information they need.

Whether a student researching a disorder, a patient recently diagnosed with a disease, or an individual who simply wants to learn more about a particular disease or disorder, a reader who turns to Perspectives on Diseases and Disorders will find a wealth of information in each volume that offers not only basic information, but also vigorous debate from multiple perspectives.

INTRODUCTION

Asperger syndrome—also referred to as Asperger's syndrome, Asperger's disorder, or simply AS—is an autism spectrum disorder involving difficulties in social interaction, flexibility of thought and imagination, and repetitive behavior and interests. Unlike most autistics, those with Asperger syndrome do not experience a delay in language development, although their manner of speaking may be unusual—for example, AS children may speak with a vocabulary and sophistication typical of adult communication. People with AS typically have normal or above-average intelligence, and although it is referred to as a "mild" form of autism, it can present significant challenges to those who suffer from it.

AS only became an official diagnosis in the *Diagnostic and Statistical Manual of Mental Disorders, Fourth Edition* (DSM-IV) in 1994, based on research carried out by Hans Asperger in the first half of the twentieth century and published in 1944. During the brief time since it became an official diagnosis, there has been a tremendous increase in interest in the syndrome, with many research papers, books, blogs, websites, forums, advocacy groups, and documentaries dedicated to the topic. Recently a number of novels (such as *The Curious Incident of the Dog in the Nighttime* and *The Half-Life of Planets*) and movies (such as *Adam* and *Mary and Max*) that feature main characters with Asperger syndrome have appeared. Such popular treatments of the subject have helped to increase awareness and understanding among the public, not only destigmatizing the disorder but also highlighting some of the positive features that can accompany this neurological difference. As Barbara Luskin, a counselor with the Autism Society of Minnesota, points out, having a friendship or romantic relationship with someone with Asperger syndrome can have distinct advantages: "They'll be honest. This isn't someone who's going to play psychological games with you. Loyalty is a big thing. And persistence. If they want something to happen, they will keep doing everything possible to make it so."[1]

Remarkably for a condition characterized by problems with social interaction, a vibrant community of people with Asperger syndrome (or "Aspies," as they often call themselves) has sprung up, much of it centered around websites. The Asperger community often refers to people with a more conventional neurological make-up as "neurotypical" or "NT," and it can be challenging and stressful for Aspies constantly to have to deal with the neurotypical world. As Kate Goldfield puts it: "When I was growing up, I constantly felt like I was speaking a different language from everyone around me. I would have such a hard time conveying what seemed to be the simplest of things, and felt like I was constantly being misunderstood. What a relief it is later, then, to find in

Recent movies such as *Mary* and *Max,* pictured, and *Adam* have featured main characters with Asperger syndrome, helping to increase awareness of the condition. (Melodrama Pictures/The Kobal Collection)

so much of the literature on Asperger's those same very words: 'People with Asperger's speak a different kind of language than their peers.'"[2] Thanks to the DSM diagnosis and the Internet, it has become easy for Aspies to find a community of peers who understand them and "speak the same language."

Ironically, just at the point that Asperger syndrome is getting more attention than ever before, there is a distinct possibility that—as a diagnostic label at least—it may soon cease to exist. The committee in charge of creating the fifth edition of the DSM, due out in May 2013, has proposed eliminating Asperger syndrome, instead folding it into the category "autism spectrum disorder." Opinion is divided in the professional community, with some welcoming the change and others strongly opposing it.

In the Asperger community itself, the proposed change has been a topic of heated discussion. Hannah Fjeldsted is one of those strongly opposed: "I consider it to be an attack on my identity and I'm not the only Aspie who believes this. Asperger's is indeed part of who I am and I have grown to become proud of that title. I take great pride in my positive aspects of Asperger's, like intelligence, memory, and vocabulary, and I do not want those gifts to be overshadowed by merging them into a title that is perceived to be more negative."[3] Michael John Carley, author of *Autism from the Inside Out* and executive director of the Global and Regional Asperger Syndrome Partnership, also opposes the label change, stating, "I personally am probably going to have a very hard time calling myself autistic."[4]

Others in the community welcome the change. Ari Ne'eman, a twenty-one-year-old autism activist, says, "My identity is attached to being on the autism spectrum, not some superior Asperger's identity. I think the consolidation to one category of autism spectrum diagnosis will lead to better services."[5] Savannah Nicole Logsdon-Breakstone puts it more strongly: "I do not use the term

Aspergers, in part because I feel like it is unnecessarily divisionary, potentially bigoted, and quite frankly I find it demeaning of the personhood of my friends who are less likely to 'pass' as NT [neurotypical], as well as of myself on the days when I CANNOT pass. Also, because the PR [public relations] work some 'aspies' have done means that people assume that I will exhibit the same way as the famous ones do."[6]

Regardless of how the labeling controversy is resolved, or whether Asperger syndrome continues to be an official diagnosis or becomes a colloquial term for a subset of the autism spectrum, the emergence of Asperger syndrome into public consciousness is likely to have beneficial effects for the autistic community as a whole. In the words of Asperger expert Simon Baron-Cohen:

> The great benefit that comes out of talking about it more is that autism or Asperger's syndrome . . . become a bit more ordinary, like dyslexia. When we hear that someone has dyslexia we no longer recoil in shock or think it's something scary. We just think, "Well, we know that this is very common, and they need extra time in exams or need a different kind of reading programme when they're being taught to read."

> I'm hoping that autism is going to get to that same point, where it becomes quite ordinary to say, "I have autism," or "I have Asperger's syndrome," and that there will be many more resources available to make life easier for people on the autistic spectrum.[7]

Notes

1. Quoted in Kristin Tillotson, "'Adam' Shines a Light on Asperger's," *Minneapolis StarTribune,* August 15, 2009, p. 1E.
2. Kate Goldfield, "Accepting Asperger's," *Aspie from Maine,* March 29, 2010. http://aspiefrommaine.blog spot.com/2010/03/accepting-aspergers.html.

3. Hannah Fjeldsted, "In Their Own Words—in Opposition to DSM-V," *Autism Speaks*, September 4, 2010. http://blog.autismspeaks.org/2010/09/04/itow-fjeld sted.

4. Quoted in Jon Hamilton, "Asperger's Officially Placed Inside Autism Spectrum," NPR, February 10, 2010. www.npr.org/templates/story/story.php?storyId=123527833.

5. Quoted in Claudia Wallis, "A Powerful Identity, a Vanishing Diagnosis," *New York Times*, November 3, 2009, p. D1(L).

6. Quoted in Fraser Hurrell, "Aspergers Diagnosis DSMV," comments section, *BrightMindLABS*, February 14, 2010. www.brightmindlabs.com/2010/aspergers-diagnosis-in-dsm-v.

7. Quoted in Deborah Orr, "Simon Baron-Cohen: Ali G's Smarter Cousin and Britain's Leading Expert on Autism," *Independent* (London), May 23, 2009, p. 10.

CHAPTER 1

Understanding Asperger Syndrome

An Overview of Asperger Syndrome

Susan Ashley

Susan Ashley is the founder and director of the Ashley Children's Psychology Center, specializes in criminal forensics, and is the author of *The Asperger's Answer Book: Professional Answers to 275 of the Top Questions Parents Ask* and *The ADD & ADHD Answer Book: Professional Answers to 275 of the Top Questions Parents Ask*. In the following viewpoint Ashley provides a brief overview of Asperger syndrome (which she refers to by the alternate term *Asperger's disorder*). She describes emotional, thinking, and social interaction issues that people with Asperger syndrome experience, as well as how the syndrome tends to manifest in preschoolers, elementary school–age children, and adolescents.

A sperger's disorder, which will be referred to as AD throughout this book, is considered a pervasive developmental disorder. This means it causes significant problems in many areas of the child's develop-

SOURCE: Susan Ashley, Ph.D, "The ABCs of Asperger's Disorder," *The Asperger's Answer Book: Professional Answers to 275 of the Top Questions Parents Ask,* Sourcebooks, 2007. Copyright © 2007 Sourcebooks Inc. All rights reserved. Reproduced by permission.

Photo on facing page. Children with Asperger syndrome do not engage in normal social contact, show interest in other people, empathize, share interests, or detect others' social cues. (© **Bubbles Photolibrary/Alamy**)

ment, including socialization, communication, behavior, thinking, and activities.

Children, teens, and adults who have AD have significant problems with:

1. Socializing with others
2. Thinking
3. Emotions
4. Intense preoccupation with one or two topics
5. Repetitive routines, behaviors, and movements
6. Play
7. Speech and language
8. Motor skills
9. Sensitivity to sensations of sound, light, or touch

Individuals with AD are different from people with other pervasive developmental disorders in that they do not have significant delays in language, cognitive development, or self-help skills.

Symptoms of AD are seen in every setting, including at home, in the classroom, on the playground, and in after-school and extracurricular activities. Virtually every area of the AD child's life is affected.

Symptoms of AD may begin to develop as early as age two; however, it is most often recognized after the child starts school, where his unusual manner of talking and failure to play appropriately with his peers begins to surface. The combination of symptoms results in a child who is identified by others as "odd" and is quickly rejected by his peers. . . .

Social Interaction Symptoms of Asperger's Disorder

Children with AD have a variety of symptoms that prevent them from making and sustaining friendships. Each time we talk, play, or interact with another person, there is an unspoken understanding that we both intuitively understand the rules of interacting. We know that we

Asperger Syndrome: Areas of First Concern

When researchers asked parents what their first concern was about their child's development or behavior, respondents replied as follows:

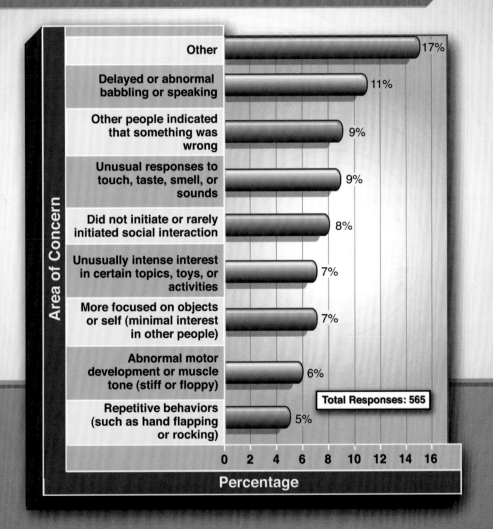

Area of Concern

Other	17%
Delayed or abnormal babbling or speaking	11%
Other people indicated that something was wrong	9%
Unusual responses to touch, taste, smell, or sounds	9%
Did not initiate or rarely initiated social interaction	8%
Unusually intense interest in certain topics, toys, or activities	7%
More focused on objects or self (minimal interest in other people)	7%
Abnormal motor development or muscle tone (stiff or floppy)	6%
Repetitive behaviors (such as hand flapping or rocking)	5%

Total Responses: 565

Percentage: 0 2 4 6 8 10 12 14 16

should look one another in the eye, listen and respond to what the other person has to say, stick to the conversation, take turns, and share in the other person's excitement. The child with AD, however, does not know what the rules are and, even when repeatedly taught them, has little or no interest in following them and does not understand their purpose.

The AD child does not:

- Engage in normal eye contact
- Show much interest in other people
- Display empathy for other people
- Share in the interests and achievements of others
- Understand body language
- Converse on topic
- Respond to what others are saying
- Read social cues

The AD child is not on the same social page as others. He is highly self-focused and has little interest in others. He seems blind to the idea that others have thoughts, feelings, and interests that they too want to share.

Thinking Problems Seen in Asperger's Disorder

Much of the difficulty AD children and teens have stems from their problems in thinking. Despite the vast majority of those with AD having average to above average intelligence, all have significant thinking problems. They are excellent in thinking about things but extremely poor in thinking about people. They have an inability to understand what is going on in the minds of others. They lack empathy and are unable to understand how other people feel and how they might react to their words and behavior. Thinking problems seen in AD include:

- Unaware of other's feelings
- Inability to read other people's intentions
- Viewing things in black-and-white

- Inability to see another person's perspective
- Rigid adherence to rules
- Inability to tell what others are thinking
- Perfectionistic thinking
- Interpreting others' words literally
- Catastrophic thinking
- Rigid thinking
- Perseverative thinking
- Failure to generalize

Emotional Problems Seen in Asperger's Disorder

The AD child has difficulties with emotions in several ways. She has difficulty understanding emotion and controlling how she expresses her feelings, and does not understand how other people feel.

Toddlers with Asperger syndrome may seem normal at home, but once they enter preschool they typically display inappropriate behaviors, such as being loud, silly, aggressive, or socially withdrawn. **(Ellen B. Senisi/Photo Researchers, Inc.)**

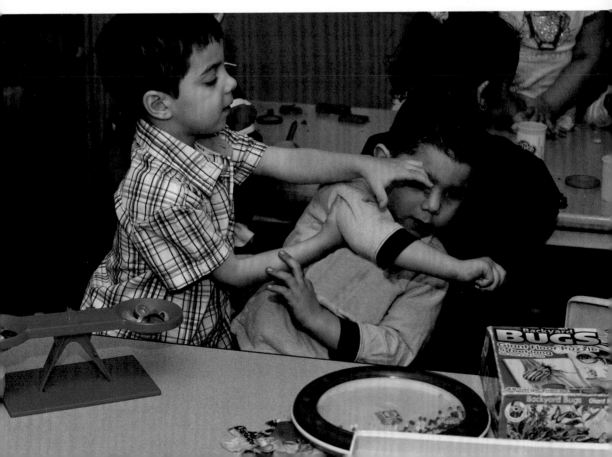

Difficulty with emotions includes:

• Difficulty reading facial expressions
• Limited use of facial expressions
• Lack of empathy
• Blind to the feelings of others

The AD child seems to move through life as if she is the only one who has feelings. Her emotion at any given time is what matters to her, regardless of what is happening around her. It is not that she is purposely uncaring, callous, or coldhearted; she simply cannot walk in another person's emotional shoes. If a peer is talking about the death of his pet over the weekend, the AD child will interrupt to talk about her visit to the airplane show. The AD child cannot understand why she should let the other boy talk about his grief and forgo her talk about the airplane show. She will interrupt, show obvious signs of being impatient, and repeatedly ask if it is her turn yet. This type of self-centeredness, lack of empathy, and selfishness works quickly to get her rejected as a friend. . . .

Daily Life of a Child with Asperger's Disorder

AD children and teens are average or bright intellectually, but they are perceived by others to be odd socially. They are self-focused and show little awareness or interest in others except for having an audience to talk to about their very specific and narrow interests. The AD child talks to and lectures rather than conversing with others. He does not like to listen, and once others are done talking, he does not respond to what they said but restarts where he left off in his monologue.

AD children have trouble with eye contact, body language, and the give and take of conversations and relationships. Often extremely interested in one or two subjects, they will focus most of their energy and conversation around that topic. They do not understand how to behave towards others; they miss out on nonverbal cues because they do not understand facial expressions, gestures, and body language. They fail to consider what others might need and instead focus on their own thoughts, feelings, and desires. They dominate conversations and become frustrated when others interrupt or try to change the subject. They cannot shift gears in conversations or activities without upset.

The Preschool Child with Asperger's Disorder

Toddlers with AD may seem normal in the home. However, once they enter preschool, symptoms of AD begin to surface when they fail to initiate play with their peers and seem content to be "in their own world." They interact better with their teachers than their peers. Odd behaviors of being silly, loud, aggressive, or socially withdrawn are frequently seen in preschool. Hyperactivity, inattention, and emotional outbursts are not surprising and can make distinguishing between AD and Attention Deficit Hyperactivity Disorder (ADHD) difficult.

Transitioning from one activity to another often results in difficulties. Repetitive motor movements may be seen as well. You may observe her excellent memory skills, with the child able to recite dialogue from favorite cartoons and movies. Enthusiasm for collecting certain toys or objects is often seen. Even at this young age, the focus of the collection is more on organizing, counting, or moving the objects rather than playing with them. Accelerated language development is generally seen and young AD children often impress adults as remarkably verbal, bright, and adultlike in the way they speak. However, they simultaneously have trouble with keeping the volume of their voice appropriate for

> ## FAST FACT
>
> A 2010 study in the *Journal of Child Neurology* found differences in brain structure between patients with Asperger syndrome and those with autism, supporting the idea that they are distinct disorders.

the situation and having a conversation where the other person can participate, and they fail to use gestures when talking.

The Elementary Child with Asperger's Disorder

The early signs of social skills problems possibly present during preschool become very apparent in elementary school. The AD child will generally be either withdrawn from social interactions, preferring to stay by himself, or quite the opposite: he is intrusive, loud, relentless, and annoying to his peers. AD children's inability to understand social behavior can result in aggression when they misinterpret other children's behavior as purposely "out to get them," and they retaliate with hitting or other outbursts of violence.

Sadly, their unusual manner of interacting is obvious and their peers quickly learn to avoid them. By mid-elementary school, the AD child is aware that he is not fitting in, but does not understand why.

Their typically advanced intellect and reading and vocabulary skills can make it confusing for the teacher to understand how a child so smart can exhibit such immature behavior. Teachers may experience trouble getting the AD child to become engaged in activities other than his interest. Outbursts of talking back, refusal to comply, and tantrums occur in some AD children who have particular difficulty with transitioning between classroom activities. However, not all AD children have behavior problems, and their difficulties may be limited to the social arena.

The Adolescent with Asperger's Disorder

The social arena continues to cause the greatest difficulty for the adolescent with AD. In the teenage years, friendships become of primary importance and those who do not fit in are often teased and rejected, making them vulnerable to depression. Middle school has a tremendous amount of peer pressure to be "cool" and to be just like everyone else. This is hard on many children, but in particular for AD children, who lack the skills to try to fit in. While others their age make friendships that involve trust, secrets, and common interests, the AD teen does not have friends and begins to identify that his differences are responsible for why he is lonely.

Social life may improve in high school as there is less pressure to be just like everyone else. At this age, teens form their individual identities, and they view differences in a less negative light than in middle school. High school usually offers more opportunities for finding a group to belong to. Being labeled a "computer nerd" or "bookworm" is no longer viewed as so negative and the AD child will likely find others with similar interests to socialize with.

Diagnosing Asperger Syndrome and Related Pervasive Developmental Disorders

Lisa. A. Ruble and Melissa Wheatley

Lisa A. Ruble has a PhD in educational psychology from Indiana University and is an associate professor in the College of Education at the University of Kentucky. Melissa Wheatley is a doctoral student at the University of Kentucky and works as a licensed psychological associate at the Weisskopf Child Evaluation Center in Louisville, Kentucky, providing therapeutic services to children and adults with autism spectrum disorders. In the following viewpoint Ruble and Wheatley describe the criteria for diagnosing autism, Asperger disorder (also commonly referred to as "Asperger syndrome"), and pervasive developmental disorder not otherwise specified, according to the current *Diagnostic and Statistical Manual of Mental Disorders*, the diagnostic manual created by the American Psychiatric Association that officially defines these conditions. According to the authors, some researchers suggest including all of these conditions under the heading of autism spectrum disorders, due to considerable overlap in symptoms and treatment approaches.

SOURCE: Lisa. A. Ruble and Melissa Wheatley, "Autism Spectrum Disorders," *Psychology of Classroom Learning: An Encyclopedia*, Eric M. Anderman and Lynley H. Anderman, eds. Copyright © 2008 Gale, a part of Cengage Learning, Inc. Reproduced by permission.

Autism is a neurodevelopmental disorder defined by behaviors rather than by medical tests. That is, there are no blood tests, brain scans, or medical procedures available to identify autism. Instead, a diagnosis is based on observation of social and communication behaviors that take into account a spectrum of symptom expression which ranges from severe to mild and also varies with age and developmental level. . . . The complexity of diagnostic assessment of autism is increased because it frequently occurs in association with other syndromes and developmental disabilities, such as Down syndrome, fragile X [a genetic disorder], and intellectual disability. Research suggests that the prevalence of autism may be about 1 in 600 children and when combined with related disorders, the incidence increases to about 1 in about 160.

The *Diagnostic and Statistical Manual of Mental Disorders, Text Revision* [DSM-IV-TR] describes the diagnostic criteria for pervasive developmental disorders (PDDs) used by medical personnel. PDD is an umbrella term that includes the diagnosis of autism as well as four other PDDs. The DSM is independent from the classification system established by State Departments of Education. Although autism has been defined in the Individuals with Disabilities Education Act [IDEA], classification criteria may vary considerably from state to state as states execute their own discretion in developing special education eligibility criteria using IDEA criteria as the minimal standard. Some states use DSM-IV criteria, and other states use their own criteria.

Variations and Subgroups

The PDDs have some features in common. But of the five PDDs, three have the most overlap with one another—autistic disorder, Asperger disorder (AD), and pervasive developmental disorder not otherwise specified (PDD-NOS). The shared social impairments are the hallmark features of the PDDs that distinguish them from other childhood disorders. Also, instead of the term PDD, some researchers advocate for the term Autism spectrum disorder (ASD) to emphasize both the shared overlap and lack of clear distinctions between these PDDs and the fact that these children often benefit from the same services even though AD and PDD-NOS are not recognized as independent special education eligibility categories. If a student is performing well academically, problems with social interaction with peers and pragmatic language use should be addressed in educational programs. These skills are critical for success on the job after high school. Therefore, it is suggested that these students be classified under autism for educational purposes. The DSM-IV-TR criteria are presented below.

FAST FACT

According to a 2010 research study, 83 percent of parents who have one child with an autism spectrum disorder miss seeing symptoms in a second child for months or even years.

Diagnostic Criteria of Autistic Disorder

Although autism becomes evident within the first three years of life, it often remains undiagnosed until 4 years of age. This delay is unfortunate because research indicates that children can be identified reliably before 3 years of age and an early diagnosis is critical because it allows the child the opportunity to obtain specialized early intervention services that have been shown to result in significant developmental gains.

The first component of the definition of autism, social impairment, is characterized by significant impairment in at least two of the following four areas: (a) coordinated use of nonverbal behaviors to regulate social and communicative interactions (e.g., eye-to-eye gaze, gestures, facial expressions); (b) development of peer relationships appropriate to the child's developmental level; (c) active pursuit of shared enjoyment, interests, and achievements with others; and (d) establishment of social and emotional reciprocity (e.g., the ability to engage in social play for older children or peek-a-boo for younger children).

The second feature of autism, impaired communication, is characterized by significant impairment in at least one of the four areas: (a) problems in development of spoken language (also accompanied by a lack of compensation through other modes of communication such as gestures); (b) inability to initiate or sustain a conversation with others in individuals with spoken language; (c) the presence of stereotyped and repetitive use of language or idiosyncratic use of language (e.g., repetition of words or phrases without regard to meaning); and (d) a lack of varied, spontaneous make-believe play or social imitative play consistent to the child's developmental level.

The third and final area of impairment is restricted, repetitive, and stereotyped patterns of behavior interests, and activities in at least one of the following four areas: (a) preoccupation with one or more stereotyped

Diagnosis of autism is based on observation of social and communication behaviors that take into account symptoms ranging from severe to mild, as well as the age and development level of the child. (© **Phototake Inc./Alamy**)

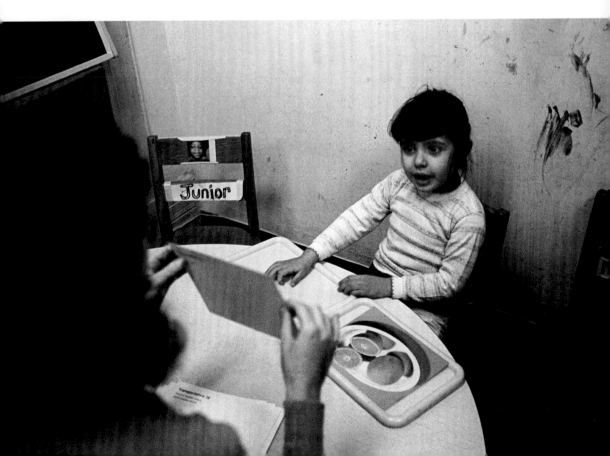

and restricted patterns of interest that is abnormal in intensity or focus; (b) inflexible adherence to specific nonfunctional routines or rituals; (c) stereotyped and repetitive motor mannerisms; and (d) a persistent preoccupation with parts of objects.

In addition to meeting the criteria described above, the child must also demonstrate abnormal functioning in at least one of the following areas prior to 3 years of

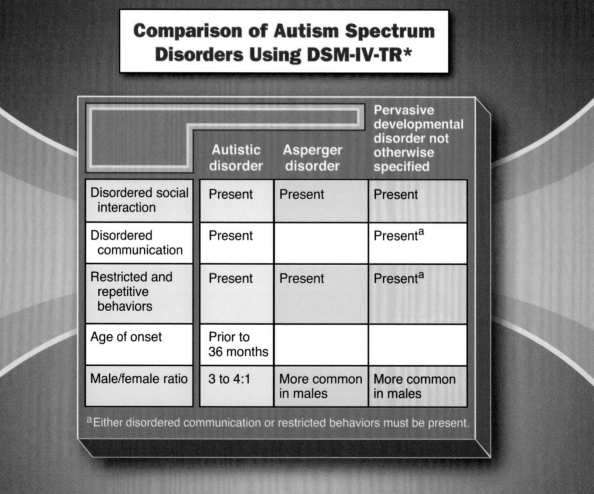

Comparison of Autism Spectrum Disorders Using DSM-IV-TR*

	Autistic disorder	Asperger disorder	Pervasive developmental disorder not otherwise specified
Disordered social interaction	Present	Present	Present
Disordered communication	Present		Present[a]
Restricted and repetitive behaviors	Present	Present	Present[a]
Age of onset	Prior to 36 months		
Male/female ratio	3 to 4:1	More common in males	More common in males

[a]Either disordered communication or restricted behaviors must be present.

Diagnostic and Statistical Manual of Mental Disorders, 4th ed., Text Revision.

Taken from: Lisa A. Ruble and Melissa Wheatley, "Autism Spectrum Disorders," *Psychology of Classroom Learning: An Encyclopedia,* vol. 1. Eric Anderman and Lynley Anderman, eds. Detroit: Macmillan Reference USA, 2009.

age: (a) social interaction; (b) language as used in social communication; and (c) symbolic or imaginative play.

Diagnostic Criteria of Asperger Disorder

In the early 2000s debate continued whether Asperger disorder (AD) can be distinguished from high functioning autism (children with autism who do not have cognitive impairment). In order to meet criteria for AD, the child must demonstrate impairments in two of the areas previously described for autistic disorder: (a) social interaction and (b) restricted, repetitive patterns of behavior, interests, and activities. The child must not demonstrate any clinically significant general delay in language and should use single words by age 2 and communicative phrases by age three. In addition, the child also must not exhibit any significant delay in cognitive development or adaptive behavior (except for social interaction), and show curiosity about the environment in childhood.

Pervasive developmental disorder not otherwise specified (PDD-NOS) is diagnosed when a child does not meet criteria for autism because of late age at onset, atypical symptomatology [unusual symptoms], or subthreshold symptomatology [symptoms not severe enough to merit a diagnosis of autism]. Children with PDD-NOS do demonstrate the (a) social impairments and either (b) communication impairments or (c) restricted, repetitive patterns of behavior, interests, and activities.

The other two PDDs, childhood disintegrative disorder (CDD) and Rett disorder, are degenerative disorders, a feature not present in the other PDDs.

Strategies Used by Children to Compensate for Asperger Syndrome

Tony Attwood

Tony Attwood has an honors degree in psychology from the University of Hull, a master's degree in clinical psychology from the University of Surrey, and a PhD from the University of London. He is the author of several publications on Asperger syndrome (AS), including *Asperger's Syndrome: A Guide for Parents and Professionals*, and is coauthor of the book *Asperger's and Girls*. In the following viewpoint Attwood identifies four strategies that children with AS use to compensate for their differences from other children. He argues that which strategy or combination of strategies a child uses will depend on personality characteristics, such as whether the child internalizes or externalizes thoughts and feelings. According to Attwood, the four main strategies are depression and withdrawal, imaginative escape, denial and arrogance, and imitation of others who seem to be more socially successful.

SOURCE: Tony Attwood, "Compensatory and Adjustment Strategies Used by Children to Compensate for Asperger's Syndrome," *The Complete Guide to Asperger's Syndrome*. London and Philadelphia: Jessica Kingsley Publishers, 2007. Copyright © 2007 Jessica Kingsley Publishers. All rights reserved. Reproduced by permission of Jessica Kingsley Publishers.

I have identified four compensatory or adjustment strategies developed by young children with Asperger's syndrome as a response to the realization that they are different from other children. The strategy used will depend on the child's personality, experiences and circumstances. Those children who tend to internalize thoughts and feelings may develop signs of self-blame and depression, or alternatively use imagination and a fantasy life to create another world in which they are more successful. Those children who tend to externalize thoughts and feelings can either become arrogant and blame others for their difficulties, or view others not as the cause but the solution to their problems and develop an ability to imitate other children or characters. Thus some psychological reactions can be constructive while others can lead to significant psychological problems.

A Reactive Depression

Social ability and friendship skills are highly valued by peers and adults and not being successful in these areas can lead some children with Asperger's syndrome to internalize their thoughts and feelings by being overly apologetic, self-critical and increasingly socially withdrawn. The child, sometimes as young as seven years old, may develop a clinical depression as a result of insight into being different and perceiving him- or herself as socially defective.

Intellectually, the child has the ability to recognize his or her social isolation, but lacks social skills in comparison to intellectual and age peers, and does not know intuitively what to do to achieve social success. Brave attempts by the child to improve social integration with other children may be ridiculed and the child deliberately shunned. Teachers and parents may not be providing the necessary level of guidance and especially encouragement. The child desperately wants to be included and to have friends but does not know what to do. The result

Age at Which Asperger Syndrome Is Diagnosed

 Ten percent of those with AS recieve diagnosis by age four

 Fifty percent receive diagnosis between ages five and ten

Twenty percent between ten and twelve

Twenty percent thirteen or older

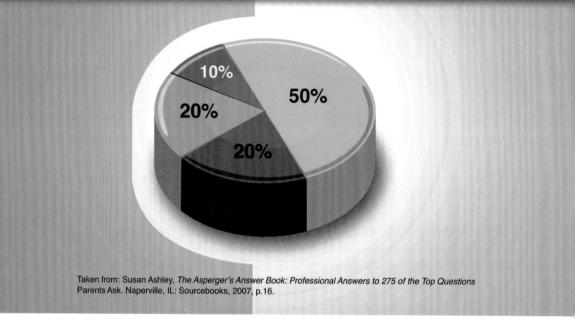

Taken from: Susan Ashley, *The Asperger's Answer Book: Professional Answers to 275 of the Top Questions Parents Ask.* Naperville, IL: Sourcebooks, 2007, p.16.

can be a crisis of confidence, as described in the following quotation from an unpublished autobiography by my sister-in-law, who has Asperger's syndrome.

> The fact is, no one likes others to know their weaknesses, but with an affliction like mine, it's impossible to always avoid making a fool of yourself or looking indignant/ undignified. Because I never knew when the next "fall" is going to occur, I avoid climbing up onto a "confidence horse" so to speak.

There can be increased social withdrawal due to a lack of social competence that decreases the opportunities to develop social maturity and ability. The depression can also affect motivation and energy for other previously enjoyable activities in the classroom and at home. There can be changes in sleep patterns and appetite, and a negative attitude that pervades all aspects of life and, in extreme cases, talk of suicide, or impulsive or planned suicide attempts.

Escape into Imagination

A more constructive internalization of thoughts and feelings of being socially defective can be to escape into imagination. Children with Asperger's syndrome can develop vivid and complex imaginary worlds, sometimes with make-believe friends. . . .

In their imaginary worlds with imaginary friends, children with Asperger's syndrome are understood, and successful socially and academically. Another advantage is the responses of the imaginary friends are under the child's control and the friends are instantly available. Imaginary friends can prevent the child from feeling lonely. . . .

Searching for an alternative world can lead some children to develop an interest in another country, culture, period of history or the world of animals, as described in the following passage by my sister-in-law:

> When I was about seven, I probably saw something in a book, which fascinated me and still does. Because it was like nothing I had ever seen before and totally unrelated and far removed from our world and our culture. That was Scandinavia and its people. Because of its foreignness it was totally alien and opposite to any one and any thing known to me. That was my escape, a dream world where nothing would remind me of daily life and all it had to throw at me. The people from this wonderful place look totally unlike any people in the "real world". Looking at these faces, I could not be reminded of anyone who might have humiliated, frightened or rebuked me. The bottom line is I was turning my back on real life and its ability to hurt, and escaping.

The interest in other cultures and worlds can explain the development of a special interest in geography, astronomy and science fiction, such that the child discovers a place where his or her knowledge and abilities are recognized and valued.

Sometimes the degree of imaginative thought can lead to an interest in fiction, both as a reader and author. Some children, especially girls, with Asperger's syndrome can develop the ability to use imaginary friends, characters and worlds to write quite remarkable fiction. This could lead to success as an author of fiction for children or adults.

The escape into imagination can be a psychologically constructive adaptation, but there are risks of other people misinterpreting the child's intentions or state of mind. Hans Asperger wrote, with regard to one of the

Children with Asperger syndrome can develop vivid and complex imaginary worlds, which may include make-believe friends. (© Carol and Mike Werner/Alamy)

four children who became the basis of his thesis on autistic personality disorder, that:

> He was said to be an inveterate "liar". He did not lie in order to get out of something that he had done—this was certainly not his problem, as he always told the truth very brazenly—but he told long, fantastic stories, his confabulations becoming ever more strange and incoherent. He liked to tell fantastic stories, in which he always appeared as the hero. He would tell his mother how he was praised by the teacher in front of the class, and other similar tales. . . .

Denial and Arrogance

An alternative to internalizing negative thoughts and feelings is to externalize the cause and solution to feeling different. The child can develop a form of overcompensation for feeling defective in social situations by denying that there is any problem, and by developing a sense of arrogance such that the "fault" or problem is in other people and that the child is "above the rules: that he or she finds so difficult to understand. The child or adult goes into what I describe as "God mode", an omnipotent person who never makes a mistake, cannot be wrong and whose intelligence must be worshipped. Such children can deny that they have any difficulties making friends, or reading social situations or someone's thoughts and intentions. They consider they do not need any programs or to be treated differently from other children. They vehemently do not want to be referred to a psychologist or psychiatrist, and are convinced that they are not mad or stupid.

Nevertheless, the child does know, but will not publicly acknowledge, that he or she has limited social competence, and is desperate to conceal any difficulties in order not to appear stupid. A lack of ability in social play with peers and in interactions with adults can result in the development of behaviours to achieve dominance and control in a social context; these include the use of intimidation, and an arrogant and inflexible attitude. Other children and parents are likely to capitulate to avoid yet another confrontation. The child can become "intoxicated" by such power and dominance, which may lead to conduct problems.

When such children are confused as to the intentions of others or what to do in a social situation, or have made a conspicuous error, the resulting "negative" emotion can lead to the misperception that the other person's actions were deliberately malicious. The response is to inflict equal discomfort, sometimes by physical retaliation: "He hurt my feelings so I will hurt him". Such children and some adults may ruminate for many years over past slights and injustices and seek resolution and revenge. . . .

Unfortunately, the arrogant attitude can further alienate the child from natural friendships, and denial and resistance to accepting programs to improve social understanding can increase the gap between the child's social abilities and that of his or her peers. We can understand why the child would develop these compensatory and adjustment strategies. Unfortunately, the long-term consequences of these compensatory mechanisms can have a significant effect on friendships and prospects for relationships and employment as an adult.

FAST FACT

Hans Asperger, the Austrian doctor who first defined Asperger syndrome, believed that to be successful in science or art, it is essential for one to have "a dash of autism."

Imitation

An intelligent and constructive compensatory mechanism used by some children is to observe and absorb the persona of those who are socially successful. Such children initially remain on the periphery of social play, watching and noting what to do. They may then re-enact the activities that they have observed in their own solitary play, using dolls, figures or imaginary friends at home. They are rehearsing, practising the script and their role, to achieve fluency and confidence before attempting to be included in real social situations. Some children can be remarkably astute in their observation abilities, copying gestures, tone of voice and mannerisms. They are developing the ability to be a natural actor. For example, in her autobiography, Liane Holliday Willey describes her technique:

> I could take part in the world as an observer. I was an avid observer. I was enthralled with the nuances of people's actions. In fact, I often found it desirable to become the other person. Not that I consciously set out to do that, rather it came as something I simply did. As if I had no choice in the matter. My mother tells me I was very good at capturing the essence and persona of people.
>
> I was uncanny in my ability to copy accents, vocal inflections, facial expressions, hand movements, gaits, and tiny gestures. It was as if I became the person I was emulating.

Becoming an expert mimic can have other advantages. The child may become popular for imitating the voice and persona of a teacher or character from television. The adolescent with Asperger's syndrome may apply knowledge acquired in drama classes to everyday situations, determining who would be successful in this situation and adopting the persona of that person. The child or adult may remember the words and body postures of someone in a similar situation in real life or in a television programme or film. He or she then re-enacts the scene using "borrowed" dialogue and body language. There is a veneer of social success but, on closer examination, the apparent social competence is not spontaneous or original but artificial and contrived. However, practice and success may improve the person's acting abilities such that acting becomes a possible career option. . . .

There are several possible disadvantages. The first is observing and imitating popular but notorious models, for example the school "bad guys". This group may accept the adolescent with Asperger's syndrome, who wears the group's "uniform", speaks their language and knows their gestures and moral code; but this in turn may alienate the adolescent from more appropriate models. The group will probably recognize that the person with Asperger's syndrome is a fake, desperate to be accepted, who is probably not aware that he or she is being covertly ridiculed and "set up". Another disadvantage is that some psychologists and psychiatrists may consider that the person has signs of multiple personality disorder, and fail to recognize that this is a constructive adaptation to having Asperger's syndrome.

Criminal Behavior and Asperger Syndrome

Susan London

Susan London is a journalist who covers psychiatric and health matters for a variety of publications. In the following viewpoint London addresses the complexities that arise when people with Asperger syndrome get involved with the criminal justice system. She says that it is quite rare for people with Asperger syndrome or other forms of autism to commit crimes, although when they do, it is usually somehow related to the characteristics of their particular disorder; for example, someone who has an electronics obsession may steal an electronic device. According to London, each person with Asperger syndrome is unique. The syndrome involves normal functioning in some areas and deficits in others, and there is overlap between the symptoms of this syndrome and other psychiatric conditions, such as attention-deficit/hyperactivity disorder. Due to such factors, she says, it can be difficult for those in the justice system to make an accurate assessment of someone with the syndrome.

SOURCE: Susan London, "Asperger's Diagnosis Is Tenuous After a Crime," *Clinical Psychiatry News,* 2009. Copyright © 2009 Elsevier/ International Medicine News Group. All rights reserved. Reproduced by permission.

Individuals with Asperger's syndrome seldom commit crimes, experts said at the annual meeting of the American Academy of Psychiatry and the Law. But when they do, definitively diagnosing the disorder and mounting a legal defense can prove challenging.

"There is some suggestion that a small minority of people with autism may engage in problematic behaviors, and that may lead them into coming into contact with the criminal justice system," said Dr. Marc Woodbury-Smith, who is affiliated with the department of psychiatry and neurosciences at McMaster University, Hamilton, [Ontario, Canada].

For example, people with Asperger's syndrome comprise 1.5%–4.8% of criminal offenders detained in maximum-security psychiatric hospitals.

And estimates suggest that perhaps 0.02%–2.0% of affected individuals in the community exhibit violence or another problematic behavior.

The types of offenses committed by people with Asperger's are noteworthy for their diversity, Dr. Woodbury-Smith said. They include vandalism, inappropriate touching, theft, indecent assault, and manslaughter.

Impaired Social and Communication Skills

When it comes to motivation, the evidence suggests that the offenses are usually related to the core phenotype [characteristics] of the particular autistic spectrum disorder (e.g., impaired social and communication skills) rather than to generic risk factors for crime, he said.

In fact, the factor most commonly associated with criminal offending among people with autism or Asperger's syndrome is the pursuit of circumscribed [constricted] interests, such as theft of electronics for the purpose of disassembling them.

Some individuals offend because they are jealous of nonautistic people, or are angry or frustrated. Often, he noted, these are "people who feel hard-done by society and by others, and are really conscious of their deficits and have gone on to do something to kind of make themselves feel better."

Other factors that have led to criminal behavior include a desire for and naivete about relationships; coercion by dominant others; and mental health comorbidities [the

Features of Asperger Syndrome That May Influence Offending Behavior

- Lack of empathy and insight into the effects of behavior; a denial of responsibility

- Lack of awareness of possible outcomes, and hence a willingness to initiate activity with unforeseen circumstances

- Impulsivity

- Anxiety or panic reactions, which may be translated into aggressive actions

- Naive social awareness and misinterpretation of relationships leading to exploitation, for example, becoming unwittingly involved as an accomplice in a crime

- Misunderstanding of social and interactional conventions or rules

- Obsessions and preoccupations

- Resistance to changing behavior

Taken from: Laura Burdon and Geoff Dickens, "Asperger Syndrome and Offending Behavior," *Learning Disability Practice*, vol. 12, no. 9, November 2009, p 17.

presence of additional diseases or disorders], such as bipolar disorder.

Individuals with autism or Asperger's syndrome who have committed criminal offenses tend to have better performance in terms of theory of mind [the ability to imagine the interior states (thoughts, feelings, beliefs, etc.) of others and to understand that they differ from one's own] than their Asperger's counterparts who have not offended, Dr. Woodbury-Smith observed. Not unexpectedly, Asperger's offenders have poorer recognition of fear in others than do their nonoffending counterparts.

This same combination of factors has been identified in psychopathic individuals. "This led us to think that maybe there [is] a group of people with Asperger's who had offended who probably had a double hit when they were younger, inasmuch as they had the risk factors for an autistic spectrum disorder but also the risk factors for later going on to develop psychopathy," he said.

Dr. Woodbury-Smith noted that Asperger's syndrome is increasingly being diagnosed in people who have committed violent crimes, but the diagnosis is tenuous at best. In fact, "this is extremely rare—most people with Asperger's syndrome aren't going to come into contact with the criminal justice system," he said, and violence is not part of the syndrome's definition.

Much of Dr. Woodbury-Smith's research has focused on criminal behavior among people with the syndrome—particularly the neuropsychological correlates of the offending behavior. He also has cowritten several articles about high-functioning autistic spectrum disorders and criminal behaviors.

Every Person with Asperger's Is Unique

Diagnosing Asperger's syndrome in adults who have committed crimes is often challenging, according to Madelon Baranoski, Ph.D., of the department of psychiatry at Yale University, New Haven, Conn.

"The psychological indicators of autistic spectrum have been minimally identified in the literature for adults," she noted. "Secondarily, our testing material does not capture the extent or the nature of the disorder."

Finally, the features partly mimic those of other disorders, such as attention-deficit/hyperactivity disorder (ADHD) and psychosis.

Work among adolescents suggests that "if you have seen one person with Asperger's, you've seen one person with Asperger's," Dr. Baranoski said. "The idea that we are going to neatly fit everyone into a typology I think [comes] from the understanding of severe autism, where the characteristics tend to be the same."

Routine psychological tests are often of limited use in identifying Asperger's syndrome. "If you give a usual battery of psychological testing, you don't get the goodness of fit that you do with a lot of other disorders," she said.

Some general characteristics of cognitive deficits of individuals with Asperger's that emerge on testing include better verbal ability than performance ability. "On an IQ test, they show verbal facility, but have difficulty applying that to day-to-day problems," according to Dr. Baranoski.

Individuals with Asperger's syndrome also become distracted by their own thought processes. "This is an interesting distinction from classical ADHD, where a person gets distracted by things around them," she noted. "It is unlikely that they will respond as well to redirection as someone with a more classic ADHD."

Additional cognitive features of Asperger's syndrome include strong ability when it comes to discrete abstraction, but weak ability when it comes to applying abstract reasoning, along with limited problem-solving ability.

The personality characteristics of Asperger's syndrome include a personality triad of obsessive-compulsive, schizoidal, and schizotypal features, according to Dr. Baranoski.

> **FAST FACT**
>
> A 2008 study of violent crime and Asperger syndrome found that in the majority of cases (83.7 percent), there was a probable or definite coexisting psychiatric disorder.

Affected individuals rigidly adhere to routines and comply with social conventions even when those conventions do not apply.

In addition, these individuals exhibit disorganization in the face of stress, overstimulation, and change, which manifests as frustration, self-stimulation, and distractibility, and they develop inappropriate interpretations of social interactions.

A Confusing Disorder

Human figures drawn by people with Asperger's syndrome or autism are childlike, devoid of detail, disproportioned, and missing parts; have "onion heads" (whereby the limbs extrude from the head); and show little distinction between sexes.

Rorschach testing [a type of psychological testing] may show results consistent with psychosis, such as good form recognition but poor integration of color and shading.

Collectively, psychological tests in people with Asperger's syndrome "present a unique configuration of findings that conflict with one another," Dr. Baranoski observed.

"It's a hard disorder to understand because they have some capacities but not others."

In the context of criminal proceedings, this set of characteristics can make it difficult to use a legal defense of insanity or diminished capacity and to explain the disorder to laypeople.

And some features of Asperger's syndrome, such as behavior that may be perceived as glibness, can prevent individuals from testifying in their own defense.

"Obviously, we need the results of more research [on Asperger's syndrome]," Dr. Baranoski concluded. "It is particularly important in forensics because if we can't explain the mechanism of the disorder, it's very hard to

expect anybody in the court or on the jury to appreciate what we are trying to say, except that [these individuals] think differently."

In her work as a clinical psychologist, Dr. Baranoski has taught in the areas of law enforcement encounters with mental illness. She also has helped to evaluate hundreds of defendants in Connecticut to determine whether they are competent to stand trial.

One of several tools used to diagnose Asperger syndrome, the Rorschach test sometimes reveals symptoms of psychosis. (Lewis J. Merrim/Photo Researchers, Inc.)

Gifted Students with Asperger Syndrome Have Special Needs

Temple Grandin

Temple Grandin is a professor at Colorado State University, an autism advocate diagnosed with Asperger syndrome, an inventor, and the best-selling author of books such as *Thinking in Pictures: My Life with Autism* and *The Unwritten Rules of Social Relationships: Decoding Social Mysteries Through the Unique Perspectives of Autism*. In the following viewpoint Grandin notes that many students with Asperger syndrome are very creative and intelligent but struggle in the school system due to their unusual ways of thinking. Grandin defines three thinking styles that tend to occur in people with Asperger syndrome: visual thinking, pattern thinking, and word thinking. She says that good mentoring and a teaching style that caters to the needs of the individual student can make the difference between success and failure.

SOURCE: Temple Grandin, "Asperger's Syndrome," *Encyclopedia of Giftedness, Creativity, and Talent*. Sage Publications, 2009. Copyright © 2009 Sage Publications, Inc. All rights reserved. Reproduced by permission.

Many highly creative students have been labeled with an assortment of labels ranging from autism, Asperger's syndrome, attention deficit hyperactivity disorder, and dyslexia, to learning disabled. The *Diagnostic and Statistical Manual, fourth edition,* used by psychiatrists and psychologists to identify disorders, requires that people have at least normal intellectual functioning, impairments of social perceptions and skills, and repetitive behaviors or obsessive interests and thoughts. The mildest of the autism spectrum disorders, Asperger's syndrome, often may simply be perceived as intellectuality and eccentricity. Most creative, intellectual, quirky students can be successful with appropriate guidance, education, and mentoring. One brilliant student with Asperger's will enter and stay in a good career because of good mentoring, but another, more neglected Asperger's student may end up depressed or in a dead-end job that he or she hates.

Many of the successful students had some formal instruction in career-related skills either in late childhood or during their teens. Their obsessive interests can be channeled into educational projects. For example, a child's interest in cars can be used as a motivator for all kinds of learning. Reading about cars or doing math problems involving cars channels an obsession into productive learning.

Discussions with many parents, teachers, and successful creative people indicate that during their formative years they were mentored. Many successful computer programmers who have Asperger's syndrome were taught programming by their parents—they were apprenticed into the field by their parents. In other cases, a professor took an interest in a student, or a friend of the family taught the individual. The best career paths emerge when there is formal instruction in career-related subjects. A mentor needs to "light the fuse" to get career-related learning started. Once this creative spark is ignited, a student

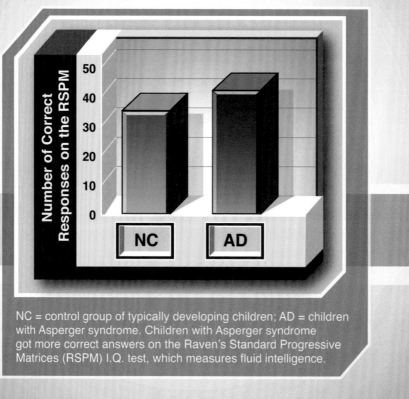

Superior Fluid Intelligence in Children with Asperger Syndrome

NC = control group of typically developing children; AD = children with Asperger syndrome. Children with Asperger syndrome got more correct answers on the Raven's Standard Progressive Matrices (RSPM) I.Q. test, which measures fluid intelligence.

Taken from: M. Hayashi et al. "Superior Fluid Intelligence in Children with Asperger's Disorder," *Brain and Cognition (2007)*, Science Direct. www.sciencedirect.com.

will often pursue study on his or her own, but in many cases some formal instruction is needed to get the student started. Otherwise these quirky, creative students may go down the wrong path into trouble or into nonproductive activities such as nonstop video playing.

One example of a student who benefited from mentoring is Temple Grandin. When Grandin was 3 years old, she had all of the symptoms of autism, such as no speech, no eye contact, many tantrums, and hours of solitary play. Today she is a professor of animal science at Colorado State University and a designer of livestock handling equipment. Half of the cattle in the United States and Canada are handled in equipment she designed. She was mentored by a great science teacher who motivated her to study with the goal of becoming a scientist.

Specialized Minds

Many creative students have problems with the school system because they are really good at one subject and horrible in another. The educational system often puts too much emphasis on deficits and not enough emphasis on the areas of strengths. For example, a teenager who may need tutoring in English should be taking college math. If this student is allowed to take the advanced classes in his area of interest and talent, he will likely flourish. If he is forced to stay in a boring math class with his peers, he may become a behavior problem. Grandin, the author of *The Way I See It: A Personal Look at Autism and Asperger's*, believes that there are three basic types of specialized minds.

FAST FACT

According to the Autism Society, most people with Asperger syndrome have average to above-average intelligence.

The first type of specialized mind is the visual thinking mind. For example, Grandin thinks in photorealistic pictures, which allows her to excel in work as a designer. This kind of visual thinking can be likened to a full-motion virtual-reality computer system. A visual mind works like a search engine for images. Many visual students fail algebra, but are able to do geometry or trigonometry.

The second type of specialized mind is the pattern thinker. Instead of thinking in photo-realistic pictures, those with this type of specialized mind think in patterns and see relationships between numbers. These individuals often excel at music and math. Both music and math require pattern thinking, and these individuals often pursue careers in music, math, computer programming, engineering, or statistics. Many pattern thinkers often need extra instruction in writing and composition.

At age three, Temple Grandin displayed all of the symptoms associated with autism. Today she is a professor of animal sciences at Colorado State University and designs livestock handling equipment. (John Epperson, The Denver Post/AP Images)

The third type of specialized mind is a word thinker who has no visual or drawing skills. In school their favorite subject is often history. These people often memorize incredible amounts of information about their favorite topics. These topics range from sports statistics to politics. Some of these individuals make excellent journalists. They have strong writing skills for factual information, but may be poor at fiction writing. Jobs that require meticulous record keeping, such as librarian or archivist, are ideal.

The Role of Mentoring

Many educators have little contact with technical fields, and they do not know of the great opportunities that exist for students with Asperger's or Asperger's-like behaviors. What many people do not realize is that mentors who could "light the fuse" and get these students motivated are easy to find. A mentor might be a next-door neighbor who is a retired engineer, or a church organist who could teach a student music.

Inquisitive minds need to be nurtured and they need direction to get started on the right path. If Mr. Carlock, the science teacher, had not entered Grandin's life during her teenage years, she would probably not be a college professor today.

CHAPTER 2

Controversies About Asperger Syndrome

Vaccines Do Not Cause Autism

Massimo Pigliucci

Massimo Pigliucci is a professor of philosophy at the City University of New York. He received a doctorate in genetics from the University of Ferrara in Italy, a PhD in botany from the University of Connecticut, and a PhD in philosophy of science from the University of Tennessee. Pigliucci is the author of *Nonsense on Stilts: How to Tell Science from Bunk*. In the following viewpoint Pigliucci argues that it has been decisively proved by the scientific community that vaccines do not cause autism. He says that the idea that vaccines cause autism was based on a biased and flawed paper by Andrew Wakefield, which has been retracted by the journal that published it and disowned by most of Wakefield's coauthors. According to Pigliucci, various profiteers and media figures have spread the false idea of a vaccine-autism link, despite clear evidence that contradicts the hypothesis.

Photo on facing page. The measles, mumps, and rubella vaccine is controversial because some studies suggest a link between the vaccine and autism spectrum disorders. (Tek Image/Photo Researchers, Inc.)

SOURCE: Massimo Pigliucci, "Vaccines Do Not Cause Autism," http://rationallyspeaking.blogspot.com, June 30, 2009. Copyright © 2009. Reproduced by permission of the author.

"The evidence is in. The scientific community has reached a clear consensus that vaccines don't cause autism. There is no controversy." So begins an in-depth discussion of the vaccines-cause-autism nonsense penned by "SkepDoc" Harriet Hall in a recent issue of *eSkeptic*. It is a must read for any thinking person who has been baffled by the likes of Jenny McCarthy and her unconscionable sponsors, boyfriend Jim Carrey (who bankrolls McCarthy's dangerous ignorance) and Oprah Winfrey (who provides McCarthy with television time so that she can endanger the lives of even more children).

The SkepDoc helpfully traces the history of this pseudoscientific tale, dividing it into three acts.

The Origin of a False Claim

The original claim came from a British doctor named Andrew Wakefield, who in 1998 published an article in the prestigious medical journal the *Lancet*, proposing that the MMR (measles, mumps and rubella) vaccine may cause autism because 8 of 10 autistic children he had examined seemed to have developed their autistic symptoms immediately after having been vaccinated, according to their parents.

If this sounds like pretty flimsy evidence, it is: the paper was eventually retracted by the journal and by most of Wakefield's co-authors. It turned out that the doctor did not use any controls at all, ignored negative virological studies that had disproved his thesis even before the publication of the paper, had undisclosed financial conflicts of interest in the matter (he was paid by the lawyers of some of the families whose children he used in his research), and had violated ethical rules of conduct (he bought blood by bribing the children at a birthday party).

Moreover, Wakefield's findings could not be replicated by other studies, so you'd think that would be the end of the story. Nope: The bastard—once charged by the

British General Medical Council with professional mis-conduct—simply moved to the United States, where he is happily making money by working in an autism clinic. As a result of Wakefield's unconscionable "study," vaccination rates in the UK dropped, cases of measles went up, and children died.

Pseudoscience can kill.

Phase two of the craze, according to Dr. Hall, can be traced back to legislation passed (also in 1998) with the aim of reducing the total amount of mercury that children get through the thimerosal that was used in vaccinations. The intention was good, though it turns out that the dangerous form of mercury is methylmercury, not the ethylmercury found in vaccines. Accordingly, the law was not prompted by any published research or serious assessment conducted by the Environmental Protection Agency.

British doctor Andrew Wakefield published an article in the medical journal *Lancet* saying that the measles, mumps, and rubella vaccine may cause autism. His research methods came under heavy attack from other doctors. (**Anthony Devlin/AP Images**)

Evidence Does Not Support an Autism-Vaccine Link

Instead, two mothers (!!) conducted their own "research" and claimed that the symptoms of autism are identical to those induced by mercury poisoning. As Hall points out, this is simply false, period. At any rate, thimerosal was eliminated from vaccines in 1999. You would therefore expect the rate of autism to have gone significantly down as a result, if the hypothesis of a causal link were somehow correct.

It didn't, in fact, it went up.

Moreover, a dangerous cottage industry of people selling crackpot remedies against mercury poisoning has

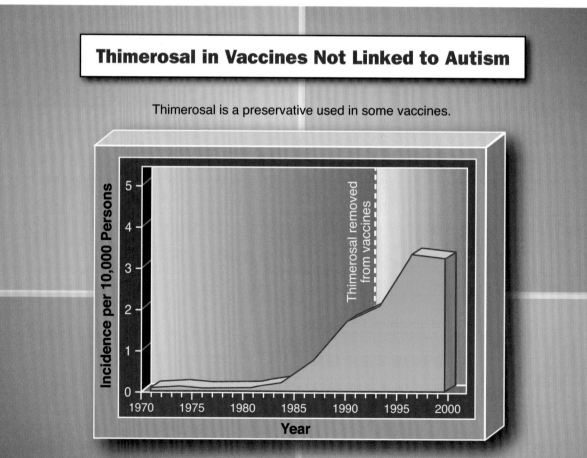

Thimerosal in Vaccines Not Linked to Autism

Thimerosal is a preservative used in some vaccines.

Taken from: *Discover Magazine*, "Vaccines Do Not Cause Autism!" http://blogs.discovermagazine.com/bad astronomy/2008/05/12/vaccines-do-not-cause-autism.

emerged, with quacks like Mark and David Geier selling a method that amounts to a very painful process of chemical castration for the hefty sum of $5000–6000 a month.

Pseudoscience can hurt, badly.

The third phase of this saga identified by Hall is the one that has seen the above-mentioned McCarthy and Winfrey involved, among others, and it is the even broader (and even less substantiated) claim that *all* vaccines produced by "Big Pharma" are harmful and are causing an epidemic of autism.

McCarthy has an autistic child, and of course she is absolutely convinced that her motherly instincts trump science. She apparently realizes the dire consequences of what she is doing, if somewhat dimly. Here is a quote by McCarthy from the *eSkeptic* article: "I do believe sadly it's going to take some diseases coming back to realize that we need to change and develop vaccines that are safe. If the vaccine companies are not listening to us, it's their f---ing fault that the diseases are coming back. They're making a product that's shit."

> **FAST FACT**
>
> In February 2009 the US Court of Federal Claims in Washington, DC, ruled in three significant test cases that there is no link between thimerosal-containing vaccines and autism spectrum disorders.

Vaccines Are as Safe as They Can Be

The problem is, of course, that current vaccines are in fact as safe as vaccines are going to be, and the dangers are only in Miss McCarthy's deranged mind. (Incidentally, there seems to be a reliable claim that McCarthy's son developed autistic symptoms *before* he was vaccinated, thereby putting in question either the mother's "instincts" or her good faith.)

Pseudoscience can make you a celebrity, the health of the children be damned.

Dr. Hall very appropriately quotes [eighteenth-century writer] Jonathan Swift in the context of this discussion: "Falsehood flies, and the truth comes limping after." That, of course, is true for the lies of pseudoscience as much as for those of politics (which was Swift's main concern). What is astounding and deeply disturbing to me is that America seems to be enthralled with this manufactured controversy about science: a substantial portion of the public is convinced that vaccines are bad, while scientists agree that they are as safe as they can be; half of the public thinks that global warming is a myth, while the overwhelming majority of competent scientists keep telling us that we are in dire straits that are getting more and more dire; and of course more than half of Americans reject evolution, despite the fact that the theory has been accepted in science since the end of the 19th century.

There is no simple solution to this problem, though these "controversies" are making the American population more ignorant (evolution), sick (vaccines) and environmentally unconscionable (global warming) than ever. Scientists and science educators need to do their part to counter this nonsense, of course.

But celebrities like Carey and Winfrey ought to stop promoting bullshit because they are sleeping with a nutcase or out of a misplaced sense of wanting to help others from the dangerous depths of sheer ignorance. And of course the public at large has a duty to society to be informed and attempt to make the best decisions based on the most reliable sources of evidence.

The information is out there, people, just use your brains.

Vaccines Can Cause Asperger Syndrome, Autism, and Related Conditions

Steven Higgs

Steven Higgs is an adjunct lecturer at the Indiana University School of Journalism and author of the *Autism and the Indiana Environment Blog*. In the following viewpoint Higgs argues that industrial chemicals in vaccines—such as mercury and aluminum, both known to be toxic to the human nervous system—have contributed to an epidemic increase in autism during the past two decades. He supports his argument by tracing parallels between the use of vaccines and the emergence and rise of autism during the twentieth century. Higgs claims that the number of vaccines administered to infants and children in recent times has increased dramatically, at the same time that there has been a huge increase in the number of cases of autism spectrum disorders. According to Higgs, the link between vaccines and autism is far from disproved, and more study and debate is needed.

This is the time of year when classroom responsibilities overwhelm my journalistic passions, and my writing tends to be more reflection than exposition. And let me tell you, nothing spurs reflexive contemplation like finding yourself in polar opposition to someone whose life work has profoundly influenced your own.

In my case, that someone is Dr. Philip J. Landrigan from the Mount Sinai School of Medicine, whose research at the Children's Environmental Health Center there first caught my attention in the late 1990s when I was a senior environmental writer at the Indiana Department of Environmental Management (IDEM). When I began exploring the links between toxic pollution and autism 17 months ago [in October 2008], a 2006 study Landrigan co-wrote titled "Developmental neurotoxicity of industrial chemicals" was the first link that Google produced when I searched for "autism and environment."

Nearly a year and a half later, I am persuaded that mercury and/or other chemicals in vaccines are among the industrial chemicals that caused the autism epidemic of the past two decades. I do not believe that vaccines caused the epidemic, but my work has convinced me that neurotoxins in them contributed to it. And in some children, they did cause autism. The question for them isn't whether, it's how, and it demands an answer.

After having followed Phil Landrigan's work in this field for more than a decade, it's inconceivable to me that anyone familiar with it would deny that proposition.

So, when I read, "There is no credible evidence that vaccines cause autism." in the abstract of Landrigan's new paper "What Causes Autism? Exploring the Environmental Contribution," I was inspired to reflection.

I initially felt he was parsing words for the publisher, the journal *Current Opinion in Pediatrics*. Given the poli-

FAST FACT

Research published in 2010 showed that when infant macaque monkeys were given vaccines containing mercury, they showed brain changes similar to those seen in humans on the autism spectrum.

tics and history of vaccines in America, it's reasonable to assume that any pediatric researcher who deviates from the American Academy of Pediatrics (AAP) mantra— The case against vaccines is closed, never to be opened again—could suffer serious consequences.

Regardless, as more than one source I have interviewed or read since October 2008 has observed, science is only as good as the hypotheses it pursues. The American experience with mercury-containing vaccines and autism is unique. And, as the studies Landrigan cites in his paper show, those used to "debunk" the notion that vaccines may have contributed to autism have not explored the right hypotheses.

Mercury-Containing Vaccines and Autism

The American experience with mercury-containing vaccines parallels the autism epidemic to the letter.

In 1930, the pharmaceutical manufacturer Eli Lilly & Co. patented a mercury-based preservative called thimerosal for use in childhood vaccines. According to a 2003 congressional report, despite repeated requests through the years, Lilly never tested thimerosal for its human health impacts. For 70 years, Lilly relied on a "woefully inadequate" and "uncontrolled study" from the 1920s as proof thimerosal was safe, the report said.

In 1943, autism was first identified by Austrian psychiatrist Leo Kanner, whose study "Autistic Disturbances of Affective Contact" said he had noticed such children since 1938.

Starting in the 1940s, American children were vaccinated for diptheria, tetanus and pertussis (DTP). A polio shot was added in 1955, and measles, mumps, rubella (MMR) joined the list in 1971.

In 1989, a fully vaccinated child of 5 had received a total of 11 injections of these three vaccines. In 1990 and 1991, two more were added to the schedule with seven

The Centers for Disease Control and Prevention recommends that children receive thirty-six different vaccinations by the time they enter first grade. (**Picture Partners/ Photo Researchers, Inc.**)

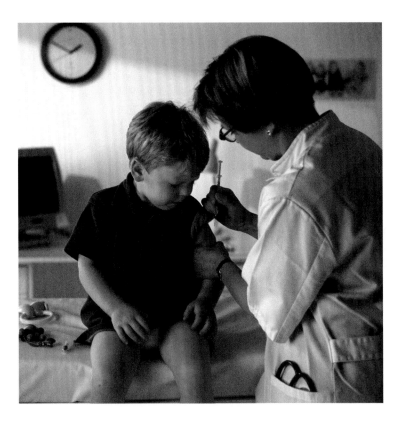

more shots, including hepatitis B at birth. And in 1995 and 1998, an additional two vaccines with five more shots were added, bringing the total number of injections to 23.

Four more vaccines were added in 2000, 2004 and 2006. The CDC [Centers for Disease Control and Prevention] and AAP's recommended vaccination schedule today says American children should receive 36 shots before they enter first grade, the most aggressive vaccination schedule in the world.

Canada is a distant second with 28, according to a 2009 study published by Generation Rescue titled "Autism and vaccines around the world." The average number of vaccinations among 30 industrialized countries is 18.

Meanwhile, between 1980 and 1994, the incidence of California children with autism jumped 373 percent, from 1 in every 2,272 live births to 1 in 480, according to a 2001 study published in the *Journal of the American Medical Association.*

Dramatic Increases in Autism Cases

Three Centers for Disease Control studies of children born in 1992, 1994 and 1996—after physicians began immunizing children at birth with vaccines containing mercury and aluminum—showed continued, alarming increases at multiple sites nationwide. The first two, published in 2007, showed the autism rate had jumped to 1 in 150. The second, published in December 2009, put the figure at 1 in 110.

A CDC survey of parents released in October 2009 said 1 in 90 has a child on the autism spectrum.

In a move that some have called an example of the "precautionary principle," the AAP and U.S. Public Health Service issued a joint statement in 1999 that said "thimerosal-containing vaccines should be removed as soon as possible." The precautionary principle actually says chemicals should be considered guilty until proven innocent, not innocent until proven guilty, as happened here.

A letter from a U.S. Food and Drug Administration associate commissioner to U.S. Rep. Dave Weldon, R-Fla., dated June 18, 2003, said drug companies had reported that the last of the thimerosal vaccines in circulation had expiration dates in 2002. Anecdotal evidence from parents, however, suggests that children still received thimerosal-containing vaccines in 2003.

Some vaccines in use today, annual flu shots and the H1N1, for example, still contain mercury.

Not every vaccine used during the thimerosal era contained mercury. But most did, along with aluminum, another potent neurotoxin. And millions of American children were exposed to ominously large doses of both of these industrial chemicals.

Percentage of California Individuals with Autism by Birth Year Compared with Recommended Childhood Immunization Schedules

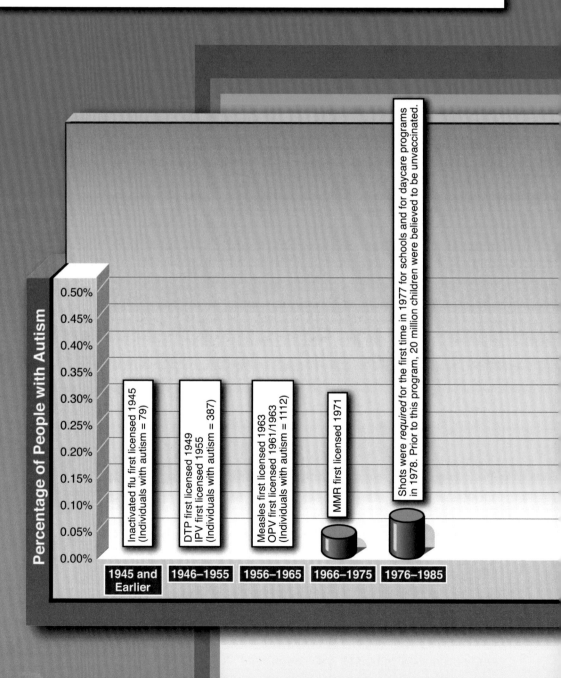

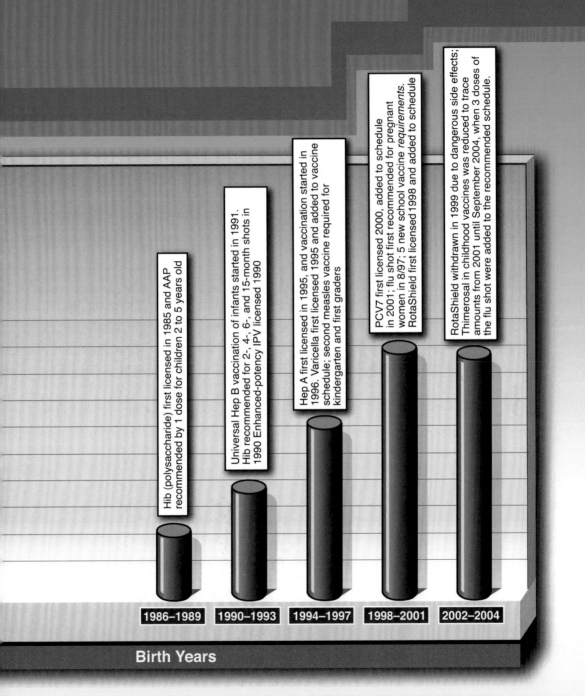

Hib (polysaccharide) first licensed in 1985 and AAP recommended by 1 dose for children 2 to 5 years old

Universal Hep B vaccination of infants started in 1991. Hib recommended for 2-, 4-, 6-, and 15-month shots in 1990 Enhanced-potency IPV licensed 1990

Hep A first licensed in 1995, and vaccination started in 1996. Varicella first licensed 1995 and added to vaccine schedule; second measles vaccine required for kindergarten and first graders

PCV7 first licensed 2000, added to schedule in 2001; flu shot first recommended for pregnant women in 8/97; 5 new school vaccine *requirements*. RotaShield first licensed 1998 and added to schedule

RotaShield withdrawn in 1999 due to dangerous side effects; Thimerosal in childhood vaccines was reduced to trace amounts from 2001 until September 2004, when 3 doses of the flu shot were added to the recommended schedule.

| 1986–1989 | 1990–1993 | 1994–1997 | 1998–2001 | 2002–2004 |

Birth Years

Poisoning a Generation of Children

The post-1991 AAP schedule called for children to receive one vaccine at birth, five at two months, five more at four months and an additional four at six months.

And that, according to the 2003 congressional report, authored by Indiana Congressman Dan Burton, R-Indianapolis, was tantamount to poisoning a generation of children. "In July 2000, it was estimated that 8,000 children a day were being exposed to mercury in excess of federal guidelines through their mandatory vaccines," the report said.

In some cases, when parents would miss one of their "well-baby visits," doctors would double up the shots. Some American children received 125 times the amount of mercury that the U.S. Environmental Protection Agency (EPA) says is safe in a single visit.

And in tens of thousands of cases, like Generation Rescue co-founder J.B. Handley's son Jamie in Portland, Ore., their parents carried them into their pediatricians' offices normal and healthy and watched them "systematically decline" over the course of their "well-baby" visits where they "received multiple shots," Handley said in an e-mail.

And Handley has spoken to hundreds of parents who shared the experience of Congressman Burton, who watched his grandson immediately and permanently regress into autism. In a speech on the House [of Representatives] floor in 2002, Burton described the experience: "He actually got nine shots in one day, seven of which had mercury.

Two days later he was banging his head against the wall, flapping his arms, had chronic diarrhea and constipation at the same time, and we lost him. He wouldn't talk to us. He became incommunicado."

Before addressing specifics in Landrigan's section on "Vaccines and autism," I should note that I have corresponded with him over the past 18 months and quoted him often in my stories, columns and blogs on children's environmental health. Just last week I featured the rest of his autism study in a piece called "Landrigan Calls for More Research into Autism-Environment Link." In my experience, he has been a man of few words who preferred to let his published work speak for him.

No Scientific Study Is Definitive

So I wasn't surprised that, after I e-mailed him about the no-credible-evidence line in his autism paper, he sent me the full study and referred me to the vaccines portion. When I questioned the relevance of the studies he cites to my proposition that mercury-containing vaccines caused some of the autism epidemic in the United States, he responded that no study is definitive, but a 2005 Japanese one was close.

"In Yokohama, Japan, the MMR vaccination rate declined significantly between 1988 and 1992, and no MMR vaccine was administered in 1993 or thereafter," Landrigan wrote in his autism study. "Despite declining immunizations, cumulative incidence of ASD (autism spectrum disorder) increased significantly each year from 1988 through 1996 and rose especially dramatically beginning in 1993. Overall incidence of autism nearly doubled in those years."

Autism spectrum disorders include Autism Disorder, sometimes called full-blown autism; Asperger's Disorder, sometimes called high-functioning autism; and Pervasive Developmental Disorder-Not Otherwise Specified.

The counterarguments to the Yokohama study reject its application to the American experience.

First, it's a study of but one vaccine out of the 11 that American children received over the decade and a half when thimerosal was heavily used. And, as the study itself says, under Japanese law children received only three vaccinations during the study period—measles, rubella and MMR—and in nowhere near the same doses as in the United States. Japanese children today receive 11 shots over the course of their childhoods. American kids receive 36. And the MMR has never contained thimerosal.

The Yokohama study's "Conclusion" states: "The significance of this finding is that MMR vaccination is most unlikely to be a main cause of ASD, that it cannot explain the rise over time in the incidence of ASD."

More Open, Honest Investigation Is Needed

No credible source I've encountered has argued that the MMR, thimerosal or any other single vaccine or ingredient in vaccines are solely responsible for the autism epidemic. To argue that would be as foolhardy as denying the possibility that mercury in vaccines may have caused or helped cause some kids' regression into autism, or that this particular hypothesis isn't worth pursuing. . . .

I've spent most of the past 28 years journalistically investigating conflicts between environmental victims and experts in the relevant fields. And, I can say without qualification, the victims have been right and the experts wrong in every significant story I've covered. I can't think of a single exception.

And with respect to vaccines and autism, I say again, without reservation, parents like J.B. Handley and grandparents like Dan Burton are right about vaccines and autism. The experts are wrong, and their behaviors—their vitriolic attacks upon those who disagree, their underhanded political tactics—suggest they know they were wrong.

For noble reasons, the most common argument against unfettered scientific analysis of the thimerosal era is that talking about vaccines and autism will scare parents away from vaccination, which could lead to outbreaks of dangerous illnesses, perhaps of epidemic proportions.

The most obvious counterargument is that we are in the middle (probably the beginning) of epidemics of horrific proportions—of autism, of attention-deficit hyperactivity disorder, of cognitive disabilities, of learning delays. One in six American children in public schools today receive special education for those and other conditions. I've identified school districts in Southern Indiana where it is more than one in four.

Americans need to know what caused these epidemics. And open, honest, rigorous debate and study is the only path to that end.

Environmental Factors Are Primarily Responsible for Autism Spectrum Disorders

Martha R. Herbert

Martha R. Herbert is an assistant professor of neurology at Harvard Medical School and a pediatric neurologist at the Massachusetts General Hospital in Boston. In the following viewpoint Herbert argues that environmental causes play a decisive role in autism spectrum disorders. She notes problems with the theory that autism is primarily genetic in origin—for example, studies of identical twins find that if one twin is autistic, there is only a 60 percent chance that the other twin will be fully autistic. According to Herbert, measurements have shown that there are hundreds of different chemicals in people's bodies (even in newly born infants), and there is evidence showing that small amounts of chemicals, alone or in combination, can cause problems with the development of the nervous system. She asserts that while some people are more genetically susceptible to autism or related conditions, it is environmental toxins that actually cause them to develop autism spectrum disorders.

SOURCE: Martha R. Herbert, "Time to Get a Grip," *Autism Advocate*, vol. 5, 2006. Copyright © 2006 by The Autism Society of America. Reproduced by permission.

We already know enough to take the environmental role in autism seriously. To say that the environment is involved in causing and triggering autism means that we believe that there have been new and different things going on in recent years, and that these developments have impact upon us. This is an easy claim to defend, and I will do that in this article.

To say that environmental factors can cause or trigger autism means that we have to look at the whole person and whole body, since environmental toxins and stressors will affect the whole body. This involves shifting from an older model that considers autism as a genetically determined "brain disorder" to a newer and more inclusive model that considers autistic behaviors as one of many effects of both genetic and environmental impacts on the whole person, including but not limited to the brain.

This newer model of autism (or really, autisms, since there are many kinds of autism) implies that we have great opportunities to do constructive things about this challenge. To say that there are environmental causes and triggers of autism implies both that we can *prevent* the impairments associated with at least some kinds of autism, and that the suffering associated with at least some kinds of autism can be treated.

And finally, *it is time* for us to *get a grip* on this issue. If there is any chance at all that the autism of at least some people was *preventable* or is *treatable*, then *prediction* of risk, *prevention* of harm, and *reversal* of injury all need to become top priorities. Moreover, environmental deterioration is a serious problem for everyone; understanding and handling it in autism may help many other challenges as well.

Autism and the Environment

It is often said that autism is the most highly genetic of the neurobehavioral disorders, and that there is little or

Mounting evidence has led many to conclude that environmental toxins may be responsible for autism spectrum disorders. (Susan Leavines/Photo Researchers, Inc.)

no evidence of environmental factors. However, observations about environmental factors relevant to autism go back decades, though they have been obscured in recent years by the dominance of a genetic focus. The view of autism as genetically determined is supported by observations of high "concordance" (matching autism diagnoses between identical twins) and high recurrence (increased chance of subsequent children having some kind of autism spectrum disorder after an autistic child is born into a family). In addition, a claim that autism is predominantly genetic rests on an assumption that our environment is stable and/or that we are not affected by environmental changes.

When we examine the frequently cited figure of a 90 percent "concordance rate" among identical twins (meaning that if one twin is autistic, there is a 90 percent chance that the other one will also be autistic), we can see that it overstates the case. Among identical twins, there is a 90 percent chance that if one twin is fully autistic, the other will have *some* autistic features, but only a 60 percent chance that the second twin will be *fully* autistic. While some researchers tend to focus on the 60 percent to make a case for genetic predisposition, we need to explain the 40 percent as well. To explain this nonconcordance we need to think about not just genes, but also the environment. Moreover, we also need to explain recent reports of high concordance among dizygotic (fraternal) twins, which suggest environmental rather than genetic factors....

Health Impacts of Environmental Change

Even in the face of widespread changes on our planet, some will still argue that there is uncertainty about whether these changes have health effects, as well as whether they could be causing or triggering autism. Is this a strong enough argument to justify inaction or delay? Not really. In committing to take notice and action, it is key to remember the saying, "Absence of evidence is not the same as evidence of absence." That is: a) just because something hasn't been thoroughly studied doesn't mean that nothing is going on, and b) the way you design a study has a big influence on the results you get.

Particularly important here is that we are learning many new things about how environmental exposures act upon our bodies that are forcing us to re-think how we decide what is safe and what is not safe. Michael Lerner discusses this "revolution in environmental health sciences" in his article, "Letter to a Friend Who Cares."... Two major areas of change are 1) how we define a "safe" level of exposure, and 2) what happens when we have many exposures in combination.

"Safe" levels: Recent science is showing us that chemicals at very low doses, many times beneath the previous "safety" thresholds, can cause harm—not by killing cells or living beings, but by mechanisms like *biomimesis—mimicking* the body's or organism's own

signaling molecules. The most famous example of this is "endocrine disruption," in which chemicals such as those in pesticides or plastics can, in very small doses, act like hormones, and confuse the body's hormone regulation systems Many people think that this might be relevant to autism, given that so many more boys than girls are affected and an altered hormonal environment might affect vulnerability.

Exposures in combination: We also are learning that combinations of exposures can have effects that could never be predicted from studying each exposure by itself. For example, researchers recently studied three chemicals found in the water in Brick Township, N.J., where an autism cluster was discovered. Each of these chemicals was individually determined at that time to be below toxic thresholds. However, in this experimental study, all three together damaged a pathway in brain development that each alone (or even in pairs) did not do.

Together, these new scientific developments mean that we have probably hugely underestimated the health and ecological risks from environmental exposures.

We Are All Polluted

While it is surprising how little our "body burden" of chemicals has been studied, measurements show that we are all walking around with traces of at least hundreds of chemicals in our bodies. Even more alarming, babies are now *born* with traces of hundreds of chemicals in their bodies (for more information, see the October 2006 issue of *National Geographic*). Given the new science showing that chemicals in low doses and in combinations may have significant effects that can't be predicted from studying higher doses of single exposures, it appears that we are basically all living in uncharted territory regarding the health impacts of pollution in our own bodies. . . .

In the face of all of these environmental changes, we need to consider a different role for genes than outright determination of our health. Genes related to autism may not so much cause autism as set some people up to have greater vulnerability to factors that can trigger autism. This is a model of "gene-environment interaction," and it suits what we have learned to date better than a model of "genetic determination." Right now, we know of no genes that directly and inevitably cause autism. . . .

Both genes and environmental exposures should not be expected to confine their effects to any one system in the body. Virtually all of the cells in our bodies have the same genome and many of the body's core biochemical processes (which are shaped by genes) occur in many or all of our bodily systems. Therefore, a genetic change may express itself in many bodily systems and an environmental exposure may target a bio-chemical vulnerability that is widely distributed in the body. The separation of the brain from the body is really an artificial distinction. All of our bodily systems are interconnected.

Some bodily systems more directly interface with the environment, such as the gastrointes-tinal system, which is the first port of entry of many environmental exposures, and the immune system, which deals with responses to outside intrusions into the body. From the perspective of gene-environment inter-actions, it should come as no surprise that we are seeing gastrointestinal and immune problems in many autistic individuals.

> **FAST FACT**
>
> According to an Environmental Protection Agency report published in April 2010, cases of autism spectrum disorder increased dramatically around the world in 1988, strongly suggesting an environmental cause.

Autism as a Whole-Body Condition

It may well be that the medical problems in autism are not incidental or extra problems "on top of" the autism but rather core parts of the problem. They may well be manifestations of systemic biological disruptions that lead, at the level of brain output, to behaviors that meet criteria for "autism," and also, at the same time, lead to various kinds of bodily illness—digestive system problems, allergies, sleep disruptions, seizures, sensory disturbances, low muscle tone, clumsiness and a variety of other problems that in various combinations affect many people with autism.

When people think about autism, they often think of the brain problems as primary and call it a "neurobiological" disorder. No doubt the brain is involved in producing atypical behaviors. However, from the perspective of gene-environment interactions, we need to ask whether the brain is the primary target, or whether the brain could be affected at the same time as—"in parallel" with—or even "downstream" of, other bodily changes, such as in the immune system. Perhaps the brain is "caught in the crossfire" of whole-body changes related to environmental stress.

Once we consider environmental impacts on autism, important questions are raised about how we interpret the changes we have seen so far in brains of people with autism. It is certainly true that researchers have documented brain differences in individuals with autism. One way of interpreting these changes is to presume they are genetically based, and therefore to look for correlations between genes, the regions of the brain that show changes, and the types of behaviors we see in autism. However, another way of thinking about brain changes in autism is to use the evidence as clues to help figure out what biological mechanisms are driving the problems. Recently researchers have been documenting evidence of inflammation and oxidative stress in the brain. These kinds of changes are well known to be two of the main ways that the body and brain respond to an overload of metabolic and environmental stressors. There are also other changes that have been documented in brains from people with autism that can increase the brain's "excitability" (i.e., intensity of response to stimuli). Such changes can be caused by both genetic and environmental factors, which alone, or even more, in combination tip the system in the same "excitable" direction. There are also various possible ways that environmental impacts could be related to other brain changes researchers have documented, such as larger brain size and reduced brain coordination, as well as limbic system and cerebellar changes. These brain changes and their impacts are hard to explain by a purely "genetic determination" model. A "gene-environment interaction" model works better. And since the brain—which after all is a wet organ of the body and not just an information-processing computer—may be "downstream" of other body changes, a brain-body interaction model may explain more changes than looking at the brain by itself.

The important thing to remember here is that we don't need to make an "either-or" choice between "gene and environment" or "brain and body;" instead, we need to take a "both-and" approach, and learn how the members of each pair work together.

Looking for Environmental Causes

We have sketched the overall picture that many dramatic changes are happening in our environment that may be contributing to the dramatic increases we are seeing in autism. Can we argue that among all of the environmental factors there is a single exposure, infectious agent or stressor that uniquely accounts for the rise of autism? So far, studies have not established strong support for this theory. At the same time, there may be some environmental exposures, such as heavy metals, that contribute more strongly than others. Getting answers to the question of cause is important for two main reasons. The first is that if we find out what is causing harm, we can work on preventing future harm. The second is that if we understand the mechanism by which particular causes or triggers contribute to autism, we can work on targeted biomedical treatments that halt or even reverse the injuries.

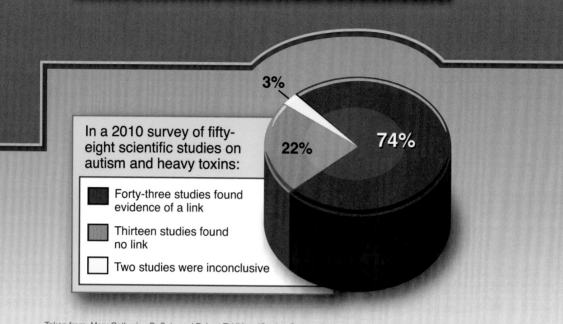

Evidence for a Link Between Autism and Exposure to Heavy Metals

In a 2010 survey of fifty-eight scientific studies on autism and heavy toxins:

■ Forty-three studies found evidence of a link

■ Thirteen studies found no link

□ Two studies were inconclusive

3%

22%

74%

Taken from: Mary Catherine DeSoto and Robert T. Hitlau, "Sorting Out the Spinning of Autism: Heavy Metals and the Question of Incidence," *ACTA Neurobiologiae Experimentalis*, 2010.

Realistically, it will probably be quite a while before we definitively establish cause, if we ever do. What are we to do right now about helping individuals in a whole-body way with their whole-body autism? How do we know where to start, given the likelihood of prolonged disagreement and debate about both body and environment in autism, as well as the huge number of poorly tested chemicals and other stressors and the essentially infinite number of combinations in which we can be exposed to them—plus variations in the timing of when we are exposed? In some respects our bodies make it a little easier for us, in that we only have a finite number of metabolic pathways through which we handle and eliminate environmental exposures and stress. This means that many different factors converge onto a smaller number of body systems, which are "final common pathways" for environmental responsiveness. From this vantage point, researching and treating the body's mechanisms for handling and eliminating environmental stressors is central to strategies for treating and preventing the impairments of autism.

Autism Recovery Is Plausible in the Gene-Environment Model

We are hearing a growing number of reports of children recovering substantially or completely from their autism. Recovery does not mean leaving behind the gifts and creativity that can accompany autism, but instead, leaving behind the physical suffering and narrowed options associated with impairments. Some of these recoveries are attributed to intensive behavioral therapy; some to intensive biomedical intervention; and many to a combination of both. Although autism has traditionally been considered incurable, the "incurability" is merely an assumption—it has never been scientifically proven.

From a gene-environment, whole-body approach, it makes sense to consider the possibility of recovery from autism to be scientifically plausible. Environmental causes and triggers are not inevitable, and many of their effects may be reversible. In particular, environmental exposures can change brain function (for example, brain metabolism, coordination and signaling properties) and not just hard-wired brain structure. Treatments including stress reduction (e.g. from behavioral interventions) as well as biomedical treatments can improve aspects of brain function. In principle, this opens the possibility of improvement and successful treatment. As we learn more details of brain-body interactions in autism, we can expect a clearer picture of how we can improve brain function not only by treating brain and behavior, but also by treating body problems that impact the brain.

Genetic Factors May Be Responsible for Autism Spectrum Disorders

Sarah Barmak

Sarah Barmak is a journalist based in Toronto, Canada, and has a degree in cinema studies from the University of Toronto. In the following viewpoint Barmak contends that the rise in Asperger syndrome and other autism spectrum disorders can be explained by various factors in the modern world that make it easier for people with similar interests and personalities to find each other, marry, and have children. In support of this idea, she cites the research of Simon Baron-Cohen, who believes that people who are "systemizers"—that is, those who like to sort things into categories and have an interest in rules and laws—are now more likely to meet one another and reproduce. In evolutionary theory, she says, this is referred to as "assortive mating," that is, "like mating with like," and reports suggestions that this may also explain the similar rise in bipolar disorders, as bipolar parents meet each other through online support groups.

M ost couples look forward to seeing their characteristics in their children. They note with glee that a new bundle of joy—generic and blob-like though he may appear to everyone else—has Daddy's eyes and Mommy's nose.

What if Junior inherits not just cheekbones and hair colour, but Daddy's Dungeons and Dragons skills and Mommy's knack for computer programming? Are two nerds who get hitched likely to pass on nerdy genes to their hapless offspring?

It was only in the last century that the idea of marrying for romantic love became the norm, rather than for reasons of economic or social expedience. Suddenly, you were allowed—and expected—to be crazy about your mate. Nay, you were supposed to look not just for a partner, but for a "soul mate"—someone who could finish your sentences, know what you were thinking before you said it, and even admire your dusty vinyl collection.

Add to that our increasing ability to delay getting hitched until later in life, the popularity of online social networking and Internet dating sites, and the general balkanization that has characterized online culture, and it's easy to see how those with idiosyncratic tics that normally would make them stand out like a sore thumb in a small, isolated town are now more able to find mates who are just like them.

> **FAST FACT**
>
> For parents of a child with an autism spectrum disorder, the chance of a subsequent child having an autism spectrum disorder is about one hundred times greater than in the general population, according to an article in Infantile-autism.com.

People Are Choosing Similar Partners

In evolutionary theory, the process is known as "assortative mating," the tendency of individuals to choose partners that are similar to them—like mating with like.

Many of us do this unconsciously and in many different ways, such as short men tending to pick short women to date, or blondes being more interested in blondes.

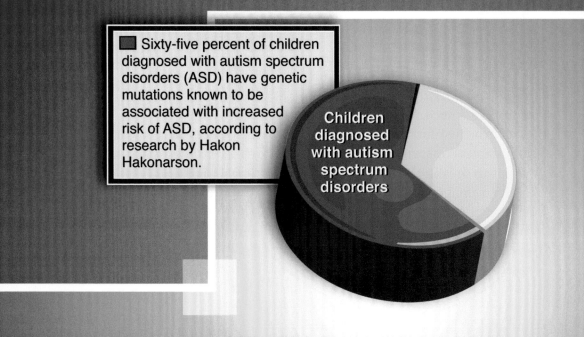

Gene Mutations Linked to Autism Spectrum Disorders

■ Sixty-five percent of children diagnosed with autism spectrum disorders (ASD) have genetic mutations known to be associated with increased risk of ASD, according to research by Hakon Hakonarson.

Children diagnosed with autism spectrum disorders

Taken from: Kathleen Doheny, "Gene Variants Hold New Clues to Autism," MedicineNet.com, April 28, 2009. www.medicinenet.com/script/main/art.asp?articlekey=99811.

(The opposite can occur too—people can be attracted to mates who are different from them.) While the revolution in dating has undoubtedly led to more couples that closely share beliefs, interests and goals, it has also failed as a guarantor of marital bliss.

A 2005 University of Iowa study of assortative mating and marital happiness among newlyweds found that the greater the similarity between a husband and a wife, the less that similarity seemed to play a role in their relationship's health.

Worse, it also appears couples are choosing each other for reasons that don't seem to make them happy in the long run. For example, people who tended to choose partners based on their attitudes, values and religious beliefs ended up with marriages with wildly varying success rates.

But our tendency to pick mates who are like us—combined with our newfound ease in finding partners who reflect ourselves in our more fluid, mobile society—might be having an effect not just on our marital happiness, but on our kids.

Consider that autism and Asperger's syndrome, once thought to be caused solely by environment or bad parenting, are thriving in the technically gifted community of Silicon Valley.

As IT [information technology] specialists began settling down in the area over the 1990s, the number of autistic children in the area tripled. Autism, once considered extremely rare, has also skyrocketed all over the world.

Simon Baron-Cohen, a professor of developmental psychopathology and director of the Autism Research Centre at Cambridge University, thinks he knows why. Autism has long been recognized as a genetic disorder. But Baron-Cohen has recently suggested that parents who are not themselves autistic, but who both possess what he calls "systemizing" qualities—the tendency to sort things, an interest in rules or laws—have a higher risk of producing offspring that are themselves "systemizers."

People with Asperger's syndrome and autism have brains that are extremely systemizing, interested in rules to the exclusion of social skills or empathy.

Passing Asperger's Tendencies On to Children

Baron-Cohen—whose cousins include a composer, as well as comedian Sacha Baron-Cohen, and might know something about shared family talents—says that a number of social factors may mean that systemizers are now more likely to meet one another and have children, such as the increase in demand for people with technological knowledge, the increase in female enrolment in engineering programs and even the rise in cheap air travel.

Parents who are not themselves autistic—but who both have "systemizing" tendencies—may produce offspring who are also systemizers. (© Paul Doyle/Alamy)

Autism might not be the only trait passed on by parents that are similar to one another.

A recent *New York Times Magazine* story that investigated the rise in diagnoses of bipolar disorder in children suggested assortative mating as a possible cause, because parents who are both bipolar—and who may marry because they are more likely to understand one another's symptoms—are more likely to have bipolar children.

And there are plenty of online support groups that allow people living with mood disorders to find one another—and potentially begin relationships.

Luckily, other processes are around to discourage too much genetic similarity among partners. It has been shown that women are more attracted to the smell of men who are genetically dissimilar from them. But pheromones may count for less in an online chat room.

Whether all this means the rise of Magic Cards among grade school kids in the 1990s means a spike in technology-obsessed babies in the coming decade is yet to be seen.

More Understanding and Acceptance Is Needed for People with Asperger Syndrome

Lynne Soraya

Lynne Soraya (the author's pseudonym) is a woman with Asperger syndrome. She is employed by a Fortune 500 company in the Midwest and does advocacy work for people with disabilities in her spare time. In the following viewpoint Soraya argues that those who work with the public, notably police officers, need to better understand the special needs of people with Asperger syndrome or other forms of autism. Using a fictional example of an encounter with the police, as well as a real-life account, she demonstrates how easily such situations can escalate due to the use of ambiguous communication that confuses a person with Asperger syndrome.

Mark Haddon's 2003 bestseller, *The Curious Incident of the Dog in the Night-Time* begins with a harrowing, but I believe very plausible, encounter between Christopher, a teenager with Asperger's, and the police. Reading the account shows how easily a

SOURCE: Lynne Soraya, "Autism and Law Enforcement: A Plea for Understanding," *Psychology Today*, May 26, 2008. www.psychology today.com. Copyright © 2008. Reproduced by permission.

person with Asperger's can unintentionally find themselves in trouble with the law.

In the story, a neighbor's dog is killed, and Christopher is found with the dog's body. The police are called, and in the confusion, a policeman grabs the teenager and catches him unawares. He reacts by reflexively hitting out at the officer, who then arrests him for assault.

Take an abbreviated excerpt from the novel:

> The policeman looked at me for a while without speaking. Then he said, "I am arresting you for assaulting a police officer." This made me feel a lot calmer because it is what policeman say on television and in films. Then he said, "I strongly advise you to get into the back of the police car, because if you try any of that monkey business again, you little s***, I will seriously lose my rag. Is that understood?"
>
> <<Later in the police station>>
>
> ". . . I have spoken to your father, and he says that you didn't mean to hit the policeman."
>
> I didn't say anything, because this wasn't a question.
>
> He said, "Did you mean to hit the policeman?"
>
> I said, "Yes."
>
> He squeezed his face and said, "But you didn't mean to hurt the policeman?"
>
> I thought about this and said, "No, I didn't mean to hurt the policeman. I just wanted him to stop touching me."

Clear Communication Is Needed

In this account, you can see many of the issues that can arise to cause a person on the autistic spectrum trouble with the law. In the conversation above, the officers use language and communications styles that could cause further misunderstanding and escalation.

People with AS [Asperger syndrome] are often very literal [and] do not pick up on subtleties. If you "strongly suggest" something—the literal interpretation is that there is an option to say no. In this case, there wasn't, so the officer would have been better off giving a straight forward command. "Get in the back of the police car." Also, the use of idiom here makes ample cause for confusion—if you didn't know what "monkey business" entailed or what it meant to "lose my rag," how would you react appropriately?

In the later part of this account, the character, Christopher, once again gets himself into trouble through his literal interpretation of a question. When asked if he meant to hit the officer, he answers "Yes," because in his mind it is the truth. There was no malice in his action—in his mind it was a defensive reaction—but it was what he meant to do, therefore the answer is "Yes." This part was handled relatively well by the inspector, as he asks

People with Asperger Syndrome may have very specific interests, which keep them engaged and attentive. But they also suffer from a lack of language and communication skills and, as a result, tend not to handle conflict well. (© Pete Jenkins/ Alamy)

follow up questions to determine Christopher's intent, but if the officer had not, you can see how this situation could escalate.

Last week [May 2008] a similar incident occurred in a Virginia Wilson's Leather store. A 25-year-old man named Marcus Morton became agitated when, while returning a gift to the store, he was refused cash back on his credit card purchase. The situation escalated, the clerk began to feel threatened and called the police. The situation further escalated, and the young man was tasered by the police. When interviewed, a police spokesperson stated, "All he had to do is comply with the officers. . . . He resisted arrest."

While I'll readily admit I don't know the details, I suspect that the situation was very similar to the account in Haddon's book. The officer may feel that it's as simple as "complying with the officers"—but were they sure that they were understood? As with the example from the novel, were they clear in their communications with Mr. Morton? Or did they use idiom and "suggestions"? Did they allow enough time for the person to understand what was going on?

> **FAST FACT**
>
> Studies show that people with Asperger syndrome have much higher rates of depression and anxiety, perhaps due to their difficulty with social interactions.

People with Asperger Syndrome Get Overwhelmed Easily

Earlier in the encounter in Mr. Haddon's book, the main character states, "He was asking too many questions and he was asking them too quickly. They were stacking up in my head like loaves in the factory where Uncle Terry works. The factory is a bakery and he operates the slicing machines. And sometimes a slicer is not working fast enough but the bread keeps coming and there is a blockage."

This is not unusual. A common way I would describe this, is that the brain in a person with AS is similar to a computer which has a huge hard drive, but with a slow audio and video processor and not enough RAM [random access memory]. So, like a computer can lock up when it has inadequate resources to manage incoming data, so does the AS brain when too much is going on. You get "memory overflow" when there isn't enough room in the buffer to save the incoming data until it gets permanently saved on the hard drive, so data is lost.

Dennis Debbaudt's excellent site "Autism Risk and Safety Management," states that research indicates that people with developmental disabilities, autism included, are approximately seven times more likely to come in contact with law enforcement professionals than others.

So, I would ask—please. Be tolerant, and try to understand the differences.

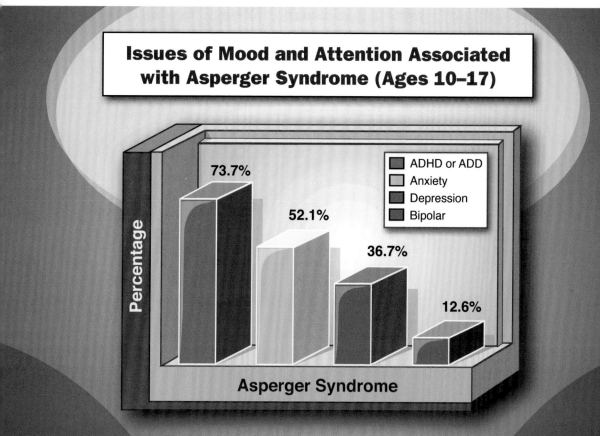

Issues of Mood and Attention Associated with Asperger Syndrome (Ages 10–17)

- ADHD or ADD
- Anxiety
- Depression
- Bipolar

73.7%

52.1%

36.7%

12.6%

Percentage

Asperger Syndrome

Taken from: Interactive Autism Network, November 28, 2007.
www.iancommunity.org/cs/ian_research_questions/attention_and_mood_issues.

If you work in contact with the public—become familiar with various ways people interact, take specialized ADA [Americans with Disability Act] training that touches on not only physical disabilities, but invisible disabilities like autism.

If you are in law enforcement, educate yourself, through sites such as Dennis Debbaudt's Law Enforcement site "Police and Autism" (especially his Handout for Law Enforcement).

If you are on the autism spectrum, learn how to stay safe.

If you love someone who is on the spectrum—learn how to help them to avoid unfortunate situations.

There are so many tragic situations caused by lack of understanding, on all sides. Please let's all do our part to make sure we minimize these misunderstandings . . . and prevent these unfortunate situations before they happen.

Asperger Syndrome and Autism Are Not an Excuse for Bad Behavior

Temple Grandin

Temple Grandin is a professor at Colorado State University, an autism advocate diagnosed with Asperger syndrome, an inventor, and the best-selling author of books such as *Thinking in Pictures: My Life with Autism* and *The Unwritten Rules of Social Relationships: Decoding Social Mysteries Through the Unique Perspectives of Autism.* In the following viewpoint Grandin asserts that having Asperger syndrome or other autism spectrum disorders should not be used to justify bad behavior. She argues that parents and caregivers must apply rules consistently and back them up with consequences for noncompliance. However, the author also stresses the importance of not punishing children for involuntary behaviors that occur due to autism symptoms, such as a tantrum that results from sensory overload. Finally, Grandin emphasizes the importance of people with autism or other autism spectrum disorders behaving according to social norms as much as possible and notes some negative consequences of failing to do so.

SOURCE: Temple Grandin, "Behavior Issues," *The Way I See It: A Personal Look at Autism & Asperger's.* Arlington, VA: Future Horizons, 2008. Copyright © 2008 Future Horizons, Inc. All rights reserved. Reproduced by permission.

Behavior is one of the most widely discussed topics of all times by parents and professionals within the autism community. Parents want to know how to deal with their child's behaviors at home and in the community. Educators in the classroom find it difficult to manage the behavior outbursts that can accompany autism, and often resort to punitive tactics, which have little or no effect on an autistic child who is having a tantrum due to sensory overload. Understanding the source of "bad" behavior and teaching "good" behaviors is a challenge for neurotypical adults who have a different way of thinking and sensing their world than do children with ASD [autism spectrum disorders]. It requires adults to rethink the way they interact with people with ASD, and most are ill-equipped to do so. Abstract concepts about morality and behavior do not work. The child has to learn by specific examples. When I said something rude about the appearance of a lady at a store, mother instantly corrected me and explained that commenting on how fat the person is was rude. I had to learn the concept of "rude behavior" by being corrected every time I did a rude behavior. Behavior has to be taught one *specific* example at a time.

Behavior Rules Used to Be Strict and Predictable

Call me old-fashioned, but adults in the world of my youth, the '50s and '60s, believed in a stricter social behavior code than do adults in today's world. For the child with ASD, that was a good thing. Social skills were taught as a matter of course. Behavior rules were straightforward and strictly enforced, another positive strategy well aligned with the autism way of thinking. Consequences were uniformly imposed and expectations to behave were high. My mother and all the other mothers who lived in our neighborhood attended to children's behaviors, and placed value on teaching their children good manners and appropriate behaviors. To be a functioning member of society, these things were required, not optional, as they seem to be today. Kids today are allowed to do just about anything. The behavior of many five- or six-year-olds I've witnessed in stores or other public places is atrocious. The parent stands there, not knowing what to do, eventually giving in to the child's tantrum just to get him quiet.

Today's fast paced, techno-driven world is louder and busier than the world I grew up in. That, in and of itself, creates new challenges for the child with autism, whose sensory systems are usually impaired in one way or another. Our senses are bombarded on a daily basis, and this can render even typical children and adults exhausted by the end of the day. Imagine the effect it has on the sensory-sensitive systems of the child with autism, especially those with hyper-acute senses. They enter the world with a set of physical challenges that severely impair their ability to tolerate life, let alone learn within conventional environments. They have so much farther to go to be ready to learn than I did growing up in my time.

FAST FACT

According to the National Institute of Mental Health, applied behavioral analysis is an effective technique for reducing inappropriate social behavior in those with autism spectrum disorders.

Sensory Problems Versus Behavior Problems

When figuring out how to handle behavior problems, one has to ask: Is it a *sensory* problem or a *behavior* problem? Accommodations are usually needed to help a child handle problems with sensory over-sensitivity. Punishing sensory problems will just make the child's behavior *worse*. Sometimes behavior problems occur when an individual with ASD becomes frustrated due to slower mental processing, which in turn makes a quick response difficult. In kindergarten, I threw a huge tantrum because the teacher did not give me enough time to explain the mistakes I had made on an assignment. The task was to mark pictures of things that began with the letter B. I was marked wrong for marking a picture of a suitcase with the letter B. In our house, suitcases were called "bags."

Behavior never occurs in a vacuum; it is the end result of the interaction between the child and his or her environment, and that environment includes the people in it. To bring about positive change in the behavior of the child with ASD, adults need to first adjust their own behaviors. Supernanny Jo Frost makes such remarkable changes in the behavior of kids because she first helps parents get control of their own behaviors and learn basic behavior techniques. That's a valuable lesson for every parent, educator, or service provider, to take to heart. The behavior, good or bad, of a child with ASD, largely depends on you and your behavior. If you want to change the behavior of the child, first look at your own. You might be surprised by what you see.

Disability Versus Just Bad Behaviors

During my travels, I have observed that many children on the autism spectrum need more discipline. Many parents and teachers seem confused about the cause of some of the behaviors that surface from within their kids. Is it just bad behavior or is the problem behavior caused by the person's disability?

Teachers and parents need to differentiate between a troublesome behavior caused by sensory problems and just plain bad behavior. This is especially true for highly verbal autistic and Asperger's children. The way I see it, many parents and teachers do not hold high enough expectations for good behavior from these individuals, nor do they hold them responsible for their behaviors. My being raised during the 1950s probably was an advantage. Life was much more structured then. I was expected to behave when my family sat down for dinner. It was quiet at the house during dinner so there were no problems with sensory overload. Today, in the average household,

To bring aboutt positive changes in the behavior of a child with ASD, parents need to adjust their own behaviors and to learn new behavior techniques for working with their child.
(© Bubbles Photolibrary/ Alamy)

dinner can be noisy, chaotic, and stressful for a child on the spectrum. Music is playing or the TV is on, or siblings are all talking or yelling at one time. To my mother's credit, she was also a good detective about what environments caused me stress. She recognized that large, noisy crowds or too much noise and commotion in general was more than my nervous system could handle. When I had a tantrum, she understood why.

The Importance of Consistency and Consequences

Bad behaviors should have consequences, and parents need to understand that applying consequences in a consistent manner will make gains in changing these behaviors. I behaved well at the dining room table because there were consequences: I lost TV privileges for one night if I misbehaved at the table. Other misbehaving, such as swearing or laughing at a fat lady, had consequences. Mother knew how to make consequences meaningful, too. She chose those things that were important to me as my lost privileges.

I was always testing the limits, as most children will. Parents should not think that because their child has autism or Asperger's this will not happen. Mother made sure there was consistent discipline at home, and between home and school. She, my nanny, and my teacher worked together. There was no way I could manipulate one against the other. . . .

Bad behavior needs discipline. But parents must never punish a child with autism for acting out, or having a tantrum, when it is caused by sensory overload or some other part of autism, such as not comprehending what is expected of him or her, or never being taught appropriate social skills. If you know your child well, and understand how the various sensory and social systems are affected by autism, you'll know when your child's behavior is "just plain bad" and when it's a manifestation of his or her autism. . . .

Rudeness Is Inexcusable

Recently I went to a large autism meeting here in the U.S. and was appalled at the rude behavior exhibited by a few adult individuals with Asperger's Syndrome (AS) who were also attending. One of them walked up to me and said, "Who the f--- are you?" He also interrupted two major sessions at the conference because he adamantly opposed the notion of finding a cure for autism. Later that day, this same individual ran a panel discussion where individuals with AS talked about their lives. During this session, his manners and behavior were polite and perfect, demonstrating he was capable of behaving properly when he wanted to.

What was most distressing to me was that these individuals felt that because they had Asperger's, the people around them should accept their rude behavior—that their "disability" made them somehow exempt from the social standards we all live by. Like it or not, social boundaries exist that we are expected to conform to, whether we're members of a "minority" population or mainstream American society. To be members of a group, we must all learn the rules and act in socially appropriate ways. People with autism and AS may find this more difficult to do, but being on the spectrum is not an exemption from doing so.

Behaving Badly Has Negative Consequences

I wasn't entirely opposed to some of the viewpoints these individuals with AS shared with other conference attendees, but I couldn't help but think how much more effective they could have been in the delivery of their message so that other people at the conference would be willing to listen and consider what they had to say. Rude behavior has consequences, and in most cases, they are negative. In general, rude or overt anti-social behavior:

- is an instant turn-off to people; most people dislike people who are rude;
- makes people uncomfortable, uneasy;
- closes down channels of communication;
- results in people forming quick negative opinions about you, whether or not they are valid or based on fact;
- alienates you from others; it reduces the chance of further contact;
- is seen as individual weakness, as an inability of a person to be "in control" of his or her emotions.

Those of us with autism/AS live in a society that can be grossly ignorant of our needs, of the day-by-day difficulty we face in trying to "fit" into a world that is often harsh, stressful, and grating on our neurology. The anger and resentment many people with AS feel is understandable and justified. What is not, however, is rude "acting-out behavior" in response to these feelings, and calling that behavior acceptable in the name of autism.

The autism and the neurotypical cultures remain divided, yet that gap is slowly closing through education, awareness, and experiences. It happens one person at a time, and we each play a role in how quickly we close the gap. When individuals with AS tout a rigid belief that they should be allowed to act in any way they choose, exempt from the social rules that call for respect for our fellow man, they widen the chasm that still exists. It perpetuates a we-versus-them mentality: "You are wrong; we are right." It also perpetuates the very negative stereotypes some of us on the spectrum work to overturn: that people with AS are stubborn, resistant to change, and unwilling to compromise. While these may be characteristics of autism spectrum disorders, to put forth the notion that these are immutable, unchangeable personality traits only further supports the "inability" of people on the spectrum.

BAD BEHAVIOR That Should Be Corrected: Autism or Asperger's Syndrome Is NOT an Excuse

- Sloppy table manners
- Dressing like a slob; poor grooming
- Being rude to either a teacher, a parent, another adult, or a peer
- Swearing
- Laughing inappropriately at people (e.g., at a fat lady, someone in a wheelchair)
- inappropriate sexual behavior in public

- Manipulating adults by throwing fits at home, school or in the community
- Stealing a toy and then lying about it
- Cheating at a card game or during a sports activity

Behavior Problems Caused by Autism or Asperger's Syndrome: ACCOMMODATIONS May Be Required

- Screaming when the fire alarm rings because it hurts [the child's] ears
- Tantruming in a large, busy supermarket/mall/recreation area due to sensory overload; more likely to occur when the child is tired
- Removing clothes/excessive scratching/itching: cannot tolerate feel of certain fabrics, seams, fibers against skin
- Hyperactivity and agitation under fluorescent lighting
- Sloppy handwriting: often due to poor fine-motor skills. (Allow child to use typewriter or computer instead.)

CHAPTER 3

Personal Experiences with Asperger Syndrome

Two Very Different Responses to a Diagnosis of Asperger Syndrome

Lori L. McKinsey

Lori L. McKinsey is a senior psychologist and the director of the Home-Based Therapeutic Services Program at Bradley Hospital and a clinical assistant professor in the Department of Psychiatry and Human Behavior at the Warren Alpert Medical School at Brown University. In the following viewpoint McKinsey describes a ten-year-old boy and a seventeen-year-old adolescent, both diagnosed with Asperger syndrome (also called Asperger's disorder). She describes the journey to acceptance as being much easier for the child than the adolescent and explains how therapists helped each of them ultimately to understand and accept their diagnosis on their own terms.

M any latency-aged [from about five years old to puberty] children are able to accept rather easily how their own specific symptoms impact them both positively and negatively. (For example, a child may be gifted artistically, but "get stuck" due to

Photo on facing page. A child with Asperger syndrome presents many challenges for his or her parents, but there is also joy to be found in raising such a child. (Henny Allis/Photo Researchers, Inc.)

SOURCE: Lori L. McKinsey, "An Asperger's Diagnosis and Success in Individual Therapy," *The Brown University Child and Adolescent Behavior Letter*, June 2009. Copyright © 2009 by Wiley-Blackwell. Reproduced by permission.

perfectionistic tendencies). When a child begins to understand the diagnosis as simply a dimension of his self, he can carry that forward into his teenage years as he begins to grapple with issues of self-identity.

Jared, a Child with Asperger's Disorder

At 10 years old "Jared" was diagnosed with attention-deficit/hyperactivity disorder (ADHD), after several years of experiencing mild to moderate academic, behavioral, and social difficulties, noted primarily in the school setting or involving school expectations. However, it became clear to Jared's therapist during the first few sessions that the diagnosis of ADHD did not adequately describe Jared's clinical presentation.

Jared acknowledged to his therapist that he experienced many symptoms indicative of ADHD, including making careless mistakes in his school work, experiencing difficulty sustaining attention on some tasks, not finishing homework, and losing and/or forgetting things. However, what created the most distress for Jared was his lack of friends.

He reported that he never seemed to know what to say and when he did interact with peers he was often teased, but did not really understand why. He also reported having gotten into trouble at school on a few occasions or accepting "dares" from other children in order to fit in, not understanding the implications of his behavior or the motivations of the kids who "dared" him.

Given his excellent computer skills and the enjoyment he experienced "surfing the net" (particularly regarding all things related to the weather), the clinician (who did not specialize in Asperger's) gave Jared a homework assignment that involved researching some internet sites about ADHD, purposely providing him with some that involved or were linked to information about Asperger's Disorder.

Children with ADHD make careless mistakes in school, have difficulty in sustaining attention, do not finish homework, and lose and forget things. Worst of all, they may have no friends.
(© Celia Mannings/Alamy)

Discovering His Condition

While investigating ADHD on the internet, Jared did, in fact, come across information about Asperger's Disorder. He approached his mother with a smile and told her about what he had found. As they reviewed the material together, Jared's mother was taken aback at how pleased Jared seemed to be with his discovery. Jared said he identified very much with many of the examples he was reading about, such as having difficulty making friends and having fun with other children; having trouble understanding emotions and feelings; and feeling the need to do things in a certain way and becoming upset when changes occur.

With this information, Jared's therapist referred him to a mental health professional with expertise in Autism Spectrum Disorders and, not surprisingly, he was provided the diagnosis of Asperger's Disorder. Now, at age 13, Jared describes his research and discovery of his Asperger's as a "life changing event." He says that once he read about other kids who experienced the same or similar feelings and behaviors, and gained increased understanding of the etiology [cause] of his social awkwardness, he felt "liberated."

It became "more black and white" for Jared, who then felt motivated to learn, with the help of his new therapist, different ways of interacting to facilitate increased social success. The therapist also helped Jared gain insight into the unusual intensity of his interest in weather and to help him develop more perspective in this regard.

Diagnosis in Adolescence

Individuals diagnosed with Asperger's as adolescents, when issues of self-identity are prominent, often have a much more difficult time accepting the diagnosis. Further, given that an important developmental task of adolescence is to separate from primary caregivers, teenagers with Asperger's often struggle because they have no peer group to whom they can turn or with whom they can "fit in."

Their inadequate social skills have generally resulted in very limited or nonexistent peer relationships. In turn, this lack of social support can sometimes lead to depressive symptoms.

Tom, a Teenager with Asperger's

"Tom" was an attractive young man who was very bright. To a layperson, Tom was a typically developing teenager who was simply moody and wanted to be left alone. But at age 17 Tom was diagnosed with Asperger's Disorder during an inpatient stay at a child psychiatric hospital, subsequent to making threats to peers who had "made a fool" of him in front of other students.

Upon discharge, Tom was referred for outpatient therapy. It was clear to the clinician that Tom's primary Asperger's symptoms—extremely rigid thinking style, history of social skills deficiencies resulting in a lack of meaningful peer relationships, and self-described "obsession" with movies—interfered with his daily functioning and overall quality of his life.

Tom experienced significant difficulty relating to the diagnosis, frequently outright refuting it. It took months of weekly intensive treatment and active rapport-building by the clinician, before Tom began to entertain the possibility that he may meet some of the criteria for the diagnosis of Asperger's.

FAST FACT

The Interactive Autism Network reports that children with autism spectrum disorders receive an average of five simultaneous treatments for their condition.

The Journey to Acceptance

The key was the clinician's focus on symptoms, not the diagnosis. Given Tom's artistic interests, particularly involving movies and theatre, the therapist informed him that iconic director, Stephen Spielberg, as well as comedian/actor Dan Aykroyd, have publicly acknowledged their own diagnoses of Asperger's. That information intrigued Tom, who began researching the diagnosis on the internet.

While Tom has continued to deny that he meets full criteria, he does acknowledge the presence of some "traits" and has been willing to work on these issues in therapy. This acknowledgement alone has been significant given his extremely rigid thinking style. He has often compared himself to Mr. Spielberg and Mr. Aykroyd, using the term "high functioning" to describe himself and the two public figures. He clearly wanted to separate himself from his initial understanding of someone with Asperger's: "a retard who drools and sits around banging his head."

It appeared that having two successful individuals who shared his artistic interests was helpful to increase Tom's level of receptiveness to engage in the "work" of therapy.

In summary, helping a child or adolescent better understand his/her symptoms in the context of the diagnosis of Asperger's is often the foundation for progress in individual therapy. Children tend to accept more readily the "label" and, as Jared stated, feel liberated by it, while adolescents tend to struggle more. Utilizing their special interests can sometimes be the hook that facilitates acceptance and leads to a level of diagnostic receptiveness that allows the work of individual therapy to be achieved.

A Woman's Difficult Relationship with a Man Who Has Asperger Syndrome

Cheryl Morris

Cheryl Morris is a Canadian living in London. In the following viewpoint Morris describes a challenging and confusing romantic relationship she had with a man who has Asperger syndrome.

I am in love with a wonderful man. He's intelligent, kind, honest, hard-working, gorgeous and interesting. I want to share my whole world with him, connect with him on every level. But he can never completely connect with me, or anyone else. He has Asperger's syndrome.

Part of the autism spectrum, people with Asperger's have normal or above intelligence and are relatively socially high-functioning. Although they can integrate into society on many levels, they are mainly characterized by having difficulties in communicating. They can't fully empathize with or understand others, especially in terms

SOURCE: Cheryl Morris, "Why the Man I Love Can't Love Me Back," *Globe & Mail*, May 17, 2010. Copyright © 2010 by the Globe and Mail (Toronto). Reproduced by permission.

of reading their non-verbal information. They show a limited range of emotions and easily feel out of control if routines are not followed.

Odd Behavior Patterns

Looking back, I should have known that he had Asperger's from the beginning. We met at a local restaurant, where he invited me and my friend to join his table. Within 10 minutes, I learned he had a PhD in mathematics, was 37, lived with a roommate in a small rented flat, worked as a hedge fund manager and was devastated when his ex-girlfriend died of cancer. All of these were red alerts: People with Asperger's are often highly intelligent, austere and have no qualms about revealing personal information to strangers.

As we began dating, signs that something wasn't quite right kept cropping up: His text messages were often one-line responses to mine; when he called, conversations were more like monologues than interactions; if I wanted to discuss his oddness, he would just change the subject. He loved routines, was in bed by 10 P.M. every night and rarely came over to my (much nicer) place.

I stuck around because there was also a lot of good stuff. We took exotic holidays. He showed me his family's villa. He was sweet, smart, honest to a fault and sexy. We got to know each other more, and I was falling in love. I desperately wanted to tell him, but waited for him to make the first move. He never did. The closest he came was whispering that he didn't want to share me with anyone else.

We carried on fairly happily for another year or so. Although he didn't show affection conventionally, he showed he cared in many other ways, sharing his favourite "alone" spots around the city with me, helping and encouraging me to run a marathon, being there for me when my father was ill.

Yet, I still felt there was something missing. The relationship was stagnating. He insisted on maintaining his routines and refused to sleep at my place. We were inseparable, but I still felt we were somehow separate, disconnected.

Realizing Her Boyfriend Has Asperger's Syndrome

I poured my heart out to a friend whose son has Asperger's, and she suggested I research it online. It was an eye opener: He met most of the diagnostic criteria. His behaviour suddenly made sense.

Excited, I brought this information to him, and gently asked if he thought he may have Asperger's.

To my relief, he admitted it seemed like he did, and then asked what the cure was. Unfortunately, there is none, but patient partners can learn to communicate more effectively with each other once there is acknowledgment of the problem and a desire to improve the relationship. He later was formally diagnosed.

Sharing his situation brought us somewhat closer. I understood his need for isolation more—people with Asperger's can be overwhelmed with stimuli and need time alone to regroup. I tried to teach him what people would do in situations where he acted inappropriately (no more high-fiving in lieu of a handshake). This seemed to help him, and his confidence and, I thought, our love grew.

Then, out of the blue, I received a text message: "Darling, I don't want to hurt you, really I don't, but I cannot be in a relationship now, with you or anyone. If we stay together longer, you'll suffer more, so it's best to end it here. I hope you find a proper boyfriend soon."

I was destroyed and cried for weeks. I wondered why he was doing this: I was sure he loved me, and despite his Asperger's, I was deeply in love with him.

> # FAST FACT
>
> Those with Asperger syndrome have "mind blindness," an inability to correctly interpret nonverbal communication such as body language or facial expressions, frequently causing misunderstanding and difficulty in relationships.

What saved me was online support groups. I learned that my experiences were not unusual in the Asperger's world, and I was warned off pursuing the relationship by long-term wives of men with Asperger's, who said it was a heartbreaking struggle to constantly remind the man you love to show some empathy and warmth. I learned that leaving a good relationship cold is typical, especially if the sufferer feels it may be forcing him to change in some way he's not ready for.

Despite all his faults, I still love him and miss his company.

After our breakup, he completely shut himself off from the world. Maybe one day, we can be close again. I want so badly to reach out and help him, to be there for him, to take care of him.

But first, I know I have to do all that for myself for a change.

A Woman with Asperger Syndrome Finds Happiness and Self-Worth

Kate Goldfield

Kate Goldfield received a diagnosis of Asperger's syndrome at the age of twenty-one. She has published several articles about her syndrome and spoken at national autism conferences about her experiences. In the following viewpoint Goldfield describes her experiences growing up feeling like she did not fit in, knowing something was wrong but not knowing what it was. She relates how her diagnosis of Asperger syndrome turned her life around, allowing her finally to understand herself and discover a sense of belonging in the world.

I might have been the only one who didn't sleep over at Mallory's sleep-over birthday party in fifth grade. No matter, it was a miracle that I had even been invited. It was one of very few birthday parties I ever attended. When I arrived, all the other girls were sitting on their sleeping bags on the living room floor, talking excitedly. I felt a million miles away. I had no idea what

SOURCE: Kate Goldfield, "Normal Is Just a Setting on a Washing Machine," Autisticadvocacy.org, 2007. Copyright © 2007 Autistic Self Advocacy Network. All rights reserved. Reproduced by permission.

to talk about. My few attempts at making conversation were painful; and I soon gave up.

When it was time for cake and ice cream, I was grateful to leave that small room and go outside. I grabbed a piece of cake and ran off to be by myself, breathing in a sigh of relief as the pressure of figuring out how to be around others was suddenly relieved. I gravitated to an old tire swing in the barn, and it is there that I smiled for the first time, laughing even. I relished the way the swinging motion of the tire felt.

Mallory appeared in the front of the barn. "What's wrong?" she asked, wondering why I wasn't at the party.

No Idea What Was Wrong

I didn't know. I had no idea what was wrong. All my life, I knew something was wrong, but I didn't know what it was until I was 21.

At recess, I would sit outside on cold, hard ground reading a book. When I did bravely venture out to the playground to go on my beloved swings, it was never with a friend. I felt like I existed in a different world from all the kids around me.

In junior high, for the first time, I became aware that everyone around me was coupled. That almost no one ever hung out alone. I wondered, why don't I have any friends? In eighth grade, I was bullied relentlessly and became the queen of crying when no one was looking.

High school involved endless entreaties to my school counselor, the therapist I was seeing, and everyone else around me about why I was so different. "You're just a quirky, a little nervous" they would tell me. I made lists upon lists of why I felt different from every person around me. I agonized over my choice of clothes, my choice of music, my lack of friends, the way I talked, what I talked about.

But I never got any answers. Not in college, when I would frequently become extremely upset when I started comparing myself to the 18–22 year olds that I lived with 24/7; instead, I tried finding other interests to throw myself into, and I made friends with the professors, who were so much easier to talk to than the students.

Discovering Autism and Asperger's Syndrome

Until the day I flopped down at the student union couch to watch TV, and randomly found a *Lifetime* movie about a boy in a residential school with autism. Fascinated, I researched the subject later online, and came across Donna Williams' books. I ordered them, as well as books by Temple Grandin, Stephen Shore, Valerie Paradiz, Liane Willey Holliday and many others. I could not stop reading books about autism and Asperger's Syndrome. For I saw in them something I had never seen anywhere else in my life, something that I didn't imagine was possible to find anywhere else: I saw myself.

A year and a half and two dozen autism-related books later, I was finally diagnosed with Asperger's Syndrome. At last, I could find other people who thought like me, who spoke like me, who acted like me. I could recreate the image I had of myself into someone who actually belonged to a group, who could have friends and connections with people.

> **FAST FACT**
>
> A study published in the *Journal of Neuroscience* in 2008 found that people with autism spectrum disorders make more rational decisions, in certain situations, than nonautistic individuals.

My diagnosis came right before my senior year of college. Before heading back to school in Baltimore [Maryland], I came across a support group for adults with Asperger's in nearby Washington, DC. I contacted the group leader and made arrangements to attend when I got back to school.

Finding Social Acceptance

I ended up going to every meeting they had that semester. In this group, I found a place where I felt accepted, even wanted. I could have long, involved, meaningful conversations with group members. I could share experiences with them and have them understand, see myself in everything from the stories they told to the way they talked to the sensory issues they shared. We could laugh about our social issues, our literal-mindedness and naivete; talk endlessly about our social issues, and not feel judged. I felt at home, and no longer felt like an alien.

That semester, I wrote an article about Asperger's that appeared in the *Baltimore Sun*, and got invited to speak at an autism conference in Philadelphia about what it was like to be an adult on the autism spectrum. During my winter break that year, I travelled to six different cities where I had family, and met people from Asperger's message boards who I knew from online in every city. I was astonished how easy it was to get along with them. The glass wall had been removed, at least when I was with my Asperger peers.

Today, while I still have my problems, I am happier and more content than I have ever been in my life. I no longer have to feel the piercing pain of wondering why I am the way I am. I have accepted myself, my strengths and my weaknesses. I am a far more confident, outgoing, enthusiastic young woman. I realize now that the goal of everyone's life is to realize their limitations and gifts and find a way to live fully within them. Every person has value, every person has something they are good at. I am proud of who I am, and want to do everything I can to help other people understand about autism spectrum disorders so that other people don't have to go through the difficulty that I had to. I want to support others with AS [Asperger syndrome], and help create a world where, as a friend of mine says, normal is just a setting on a washing machine.

GLOSSARY

Asperger syndrome (AS) An autism spectrum disorder characterized by impairment in social interaction and nonverbal communication, as well as restricted and repetitive patterns of behavior and interests, but without significant delay in development of language. Also known as Asperger's syndrome or Asperger's disorder.

Aspie A slang term for a person with Asperger syndrome, commonly used in the Asperger community.

assortative mating Mating by individuals with similar traits; it has been proposed as a factor in the increase in autism spectrum disorders.

attention-deficit/ hyperactivity disorder (ADHD) A condition, more prevalent in boys, characterized by impulsiveness, inattention, and hyperactivity.

autism spectrum disorder (ASD) A term for the range of disorders that includes autism, Asperger syndrome, and pervasive developmental disorder not otherwise specified; refers to the combination and range of autistic characteristics that can vary from mild to severe.

autistic disorder (autism) A brain disorder that impairs social relationships, interactions, and communication and is characterized by a seeming withdrawal from the world and a turning inward to restricted behaviors and interests.

comorbidity The simultaneous presence of two or more disorders or diseases in the same individual.

DSM The *Diagnostic and Statistical Manual of Mental Disorders* (DSM) is published by the American Psychiatric Association and establishes the official diagnostic criteria for psychiatric conditions in North America. Currently in its fourth edition (DSM-IV), the next revision (DSM-V) is scheduled for publication in 2013.

empathy	The ability to identify with and understand the emotions and physical feelings of another person as if they were one's own.
high-functioning autism (HFA)	An autism condition in which communication is possible, intelligence is normal or high, and the individual's social impairments are not severe. Some experts contend that AS and HFA are essentially the same.
ICD-10	The *International Statistical Classification of Diseases and Related Health Problems, Tenth Revision* (ICD-10) is the European guide for diagnosis of mental disorders, equivalent to the DSM.
incidence	The number of newly diagnosed cases of a medical condition during a specified period of time.
Individuals with Disabilities Education Act (IDEA)	A federal law governing how states and public agencies provide early intervention, special education, and related services to millions of eligible infants, toddlers, children, and adolescents with disabilities.
IQ	Intelligence quotient; a measure of a person's general intelligence as determined by a standardized test.
neurological	Involving the nervous system and the brain.
neurotoxic	Harmful to the nervous system.
neurotypical (NT)	A term for people with typical neurological development and behavior; often used in the Asperger community.
nonverbal communication	Communication without words, by means of body language, voice tone, facial expression, movements, posture, touching, gestures, and eye contact.
obsessive-compulsive disorder (OCD)	A mental disorder characterized by intrusive, anxiety-producing thoughts and repetitive rituals that the individual cannot control.

pervasive developmental disorder not otherwise specified (PDD-NOS)	A category for people who have some autism spectrum disorder characteristics but whose symptoms do not sufficiently match those of either autism or Asperger syndrome; sometimes referred to as atypical autism.
prevalence	The total number of individuals in a population who have a disease or other health condition during a specific period of time.
self-stimulation	Behavior that seems to have the purpose of activating or stimulating the senses and may be a way of focusing or shutting out unwanted stimulation.
socialization	The process by which children learn the customs, behavioral norms, and beliefs of the society in which they live.
social impairment	Difficulty in interacting socially with others, due to deficits in nonverbal communication and/or theory of mind.
systemize	To organize into a system.
theory of mind	The ability to empathize with other people so that one can make sense of their reactions and behavior. This makes it possible to recognize thoughts, feelings, intentions, and beliefs in other people.
thimerosal	An antiseptic and antifungal agent containing methylmercury; believed by some to be a cause of autism when used in vaccines.

CHRONOLOGY

c. 1220   Brother Juniper, one of the original followers of Saint Francis of Assisi, is one of the earliest historical figures believed by some modern autism experts to have had Asperger syndrome, due to characteristics such as naïveté and extremely literal interpretations.

1911   Psychiatrist Eugen Bleuler coins the term *autism*, from the Greek word *autos*, meaning "self." He invented the term to describe schizophrenic patients that closed themselves off and were very self-absorbed. He defines *autism* as an "escape from reality."

1926   Eva Sucharewa, a Russian neurological assistant, writes a paper titled "Schizoid Personality of Childhood" that describes the case studies of six boys whose behavior closely resembled those later described by Hans Asperger.

1938   Psychiatrist Leo Kanner observes the behavior of eleven children described as emotionally or intellectually impaired; among some of the children, he finds behavior and abilities that do not reflect impairment.

1943   Kanner identifies autism as a medical condition in his scientific paper "Autistic Disturbance of Affective Contact," describing it as a developmental disability that affects emotional and social understanding and skills. He also describes coexisting psychiatric conditions, including anxiety disorders, in his autism patients. Kanner reports an autism rate of 1 in 10,000.

1944 Working independently of Kanner, Hans Asperger publishes a paper in German describing "autistic psychopathy" in four children. The children are similar to those described by Kanner, except for having more adult speech patterns.

1944 Asperger, along with Sister Victorine, opens the first school for children with Asperger syndrome (referred to at the time as "autistic psychopathy").

1945 Toward the end of World War II, an Allied bombing raid strikes Asperger's hospital, killing Sister Victorine and destroying much of Asperger's early work.

1970 One in every 2,500 American children is estimated to have autism.

1970s In Sweden, the first autistim classes within special education are started.

1976 New types of disability categories begin to be introduced in the scientific community, such as specific learning disabilities, serious emotional disturbances, and others.

1980 Infantile autism is added to the *Diagnostic and Statistical Manual of Mental Disorders*.

1981 British psychiatrist Lorna Wing first uses the term *Asperger's syndrome*.

1987 Pervasive developmental disorder not otherwise specified (PDD-NOS) is added to the *Diagnostic and Statistical Manual of Mental Disorders*, revising the criteria for identifying autism and allowing more people to be included in the autism category.

1989   Hans Asperger's work is translated into English.

1990   An estimated 4.7 out of every 10,000 American children are diagnosed with autism.

1991   Autism is added as a category for tracking American schoolchildren who receive special education services.

1992   Asperger syndrome is included in the tenth published edition of the *International Statistical Classification of Diseases* (ICD-10), published by the World Health Organization.

1994   Asperger syndrome is added to the *Diagnostic and Statistical Manual of Mental Disorders.*

1995   Over 22,000 American schoolchildren receive special education services for autism.

1998   In the United Kingdom, Andrew Wakefield publishes a paper reporting on twelve children who were diagnosed with autism and bowel disease after receiving the measles, mumps, and rubella vaccine. The study is later widely discredited.

1999   Citing the precautionary principle, the American Academy of Pediatrics and the US Public Health Service recommend in a joint statement that the preservative thimerosal be removed from vaccines.

2001   The American Medical Association reports that the incidence of autism in California children increased 373 percent from 1980 to 1994.

2002   Autism is estimated to increase at a rate of 10 to 17 percent each year.

2003–2004   Much-debated studies show that 60 out of every 10,000 American children are diagnosed with autism, which equals a ratio of 1 in every 166 children.

2004   Over 140,000 American schoolchildren receive special education services for autism.

2007   A Centers for Disease Control and Prevention study reports an autism incidence of 1 in 150.

2009   The US Court of Federal Claims in Washington, DC, rules in three significant test cases that there is no link between thimerosal-containing vaccines and autism spectrum disorders.

2009   A Centers for Disease Control and Prevention study reports an autism incidence of 1 in 110.

2010   A study in the *Journal of Child Neurology* finds differences in brain structure between patients with Asperger syndrome and those with autism, supporting the idea that they are distinct disorders.

The American Psychiatric Association proposes eliminating the diagnoses Asperger syndrome and pervasive developmental disorder not otherwise specified in the forthcoming edition of the *Diagnostic and Statistical Manual of Mental Disorders, Fifth Edition* (DSM-V), expected to be released in May 2013. Under the proposed revision there will be one diagnostic category called autistic spectrum disorder, which will cover all forms of autism, from high-functioning to severely disabling.

According to a US Environmental Protection Agency report published in April, cases of autism spectrum disorder increased dramatically around the world in 1988, strongly suggesting an environmental cause.

ORGANIZATIONS TO CONTACT

The editors have compiled the following list of organizations concerned with the issues debated in this book. The descriptions are derived from materials provided by the organizations. All have publications or information available for interested readers. The list was compiled on the date of publication of the present volume; the information provided here may change. Be aware that many organizations take several weeks or longer to respond to inquiries, so allow as much time as possible.

Asperger Syndrome and High Functioning Autism Association (AHA)
PO Box 916, Bethpage NY 11714
(888) 918-9198
e-mail: pats@ahany .org
website: www.ahany .org

The AHA aims to increase awareness and knowledge of high-functioning autism among the professionals who diagnose, treat, educate, or provide services, as well as to attain appropriate educational programs, effective social skills training, increased social and recreational opportunities, meaningful employment, and sufficient and satisfactory independent living accommodations for those with high-functioning autism. The organization hosts conferences and support groups in the northeastern United States, provides an e-list, and offers information about Asperger syndrome on its website.

Autism Information Center
Centers for Disease Control and Prevention
1600 Clifton Rd.
Atlanta, GA 30333
(800) 232-4636
e-mail: cdcinfo@cdc .gov
website: www.cdc.gov/ ncbddd/autism

The US Department of Health and Human Services' Centers for Disease Control and Prevention provides extensive information about autism spectrum disorders, downloadable fact sheets, and general publications. It also conducts and funds research into all aspects of autism spectrum disorders.

Autism Network International (ANI)
PO Box 35448,
Syracuse, NY 13235-5448
e-mail: jisincla@syr.edu
website: http://ani.autistics.org

ANI is a self-help and advocacy organization run by individuals with autism. It advocates for civil rights and self-determination for all autistic people. ANI also produces the newsletter *Our Voices*, published quarterly.

Autism Research Institute (ARI)
4182 Adams Ave.
San Diego, CA 92116
(866) 366-3361
e-mail: matt@autism.com
website: www.autism.com

This national organization focuses on research and information concerning autism and related disorders. ARI started Defeat Autism Now!, an autism think tank and conference group, and publishes the quarterly *Autism Research Review International Newsletter*. Its website offers podcasts, a discussion group, streaming video of conferences, and other resources.

Autism Society Canada (ASC)
Box 22017, 1670 Heron Rd., Ottawa ON, K1V 0C2
(613) 789-8943
toll free: (866) 476-8440
e-mail: info@autismsocietycanada.ca
website: www.autismsocietycanada.ca

The ASC is a federation of Canada-wide provincial and territorial autism societies founded in 1976 by a group of concerned parents. The organization is committed to advocacy, public education, information and referral, and support for its regional societies. It provides direct support to people with autism spectrum disorders and their families.

Autism Society of America
4340 East-West Hwy. Ste. 350, Bethesda, MD 20814
(301) 657-0881
toll-free: (800) 328-8476
e-mail: info@autism-society.org
website: www.autism-society.org

This organization is one of the largest autism support groups in the United States, with thirty thousand members. It provides information and referrals to autism services nationwide. Its mission is to increase public awareness of autism and to help individuals with autism and their families deal with day-to-day issues. Autistic people are among the advisers to the organization. Its website offers a free e-newsletter, *ASA-Net*. The organization also publishes a quarterly newsletter for members called *Autism Advocate*.

Autism Speaks
1 E. Thirty-Third St. 4th Fl., New York, NY 10016
(212) 252-8584
fax: (212) 252-8676
e-mail: contactus@autismspeaks.org
website: www.autismspeaks.org

This national organization promotes public awareness of autism and works to fund research into causes, prevention, and treatment of autism. Its website offers the *e-Speaks* newsletter, as well as news archives and various resources.

Autism Women's Network (AWN)
138 Sullivan St., New York, NY 10012
(888) 650-2290
website: www.autismwomensnetwork.org

AWN is dedicated to building a community consisting of women on the autism spectrum and their families, friends, and supporters, and to providing a place where they can share their experiences in a diverse, inclusive, and supportive environment. The organization's website provides a discussion forum and articles.

Doug Flutie Jr. Foundation for Autism
PO Box 767
Framingham, MA 01701
(508) 270-8855
toll-free: (866) 328-8476
fax: (508) 270-6868
website: www.doug flutiejrfoundation.org

Founded by retired National Football League quarterback Doug Flutie, this organization's goal is to provide disadvantaged families with assistance in caring for children who are autistic. In addition to funding education and research, the foundation also disseminates information on programs and services for individuals with autism.

Family Voices
2340 Alamo SE, Ste. 102, Albuquerque NM 87106
(505) 872-4774
toll-free: (888) 835-5669
fax: (505) 872-4780
e-mail: kidshealth@familyvoices.org
website: www.family voices.org

Family Voices is a national organization providing information and education about family-based health care for children with disabilities. It offers multiple publications, including the newsletters *Friday's Child* and *Bright Futures*, all of which can be found on the website.

The Global and Regional Asperger Syndrome Partnership (GRASP)
666 Broadway, Ste. 830, New York, NY 10012
(888) 474-7277
e-mail: info@grasp.org
website: www.grasp .org

GRASP is an educational and advocacy organization serving individuals on the autism spectrum. According to the bylaws of the organization, the executive director, the entire advisory board, and 50 percent of the board of directors must be diagnosed with either autism, Asperger syndrome, or pervasive developmental disorder. GRASP provides articles, interviews, and links to therapists and resources.

National Autism Association (NAA)
1330 W. Schatz Ln.,
Nixa, MO 65714
(877) 622-6733
e-mail: naa@national
autism.org
website: www.nation
alautismassociation
.org

This organization focuses on autism research, advocacy, education, and support for those affected by autism spectrum disorders. Its goal is to inform society that autism is not a lifelong incurable genetic disorder but one that is biomedically definable and treatable. The NAA also works to raise public and professional awareness of environmental toxins as causative factors in neurological damage that often results in autism or a related diagnosis. The website provides research findings as well as press releases.

National Institute of Child Health and Human Development (NICHD)
Bldg. 31, Room 2A32
MSC 2425, 31 Center
Dr., Bethesda, MD
20892-2425
(800) 370-2943
fax: (866) 760-5947
e-mail: nicidclear
inghouse@mail.nih.gov
website: www.nichd
.nih.gov

This government institute, part of the National Institutes of Health, supports and conducts research on all areas of human development, from infancy to adulthood. Health information publications can be found on the website or by contacting the institute directly.

National Institute of Mental Health (NIMH)
6001 Executive Blvd.,
Rm. 8184, MSC 9663,
Bethesda, MD 20892-
9663
(301) 443-4513
toll-free: (866) 615-6464
fax: (301) 443-4279
e-mail: nimhinfo@nih
.gov
website: www.nimh
.nih.gov

This government institute, part of the National Institutes of Health, covers all aspects of mental illness and behavioral disorders. The institute conducts and supports research; analyzes and disseminates information on mental health causes, occurrence, and treatment; supports the training of scientists to conduct research; and gives out information to the public concerning mental health and behavioral disorders. Pamphlets, fact sheets, and booklets can be found on the website or by contacting the institute directly.

National Institute of Neurological Disorders and Stroke (NINDS)
PO Box 5801
Bethesda, MD 20824
(301) 496-5751
toll-free: (800) 352-9424
website: www.ninds
.nih.gov/disorders/
asperger/asperger.htm

This government institute, part of the National Institutes of Health, covers the neurological aspects of Asperger syndrome. The institute publishes numerous fact sheets that can be obtained through its website or by contacting the institute directly.

OASIS @ MAAP
PO Box 524, Crown Point, IN 46308
(219) 662-1311
fax: (219) 662-0638
e-mail: info@asperger
syndrome.org
website: www.asperger
syndrome.org

OASIS @ MAAP is a combined project of OASIS (Online Asperger Syndrome Information and Support) and MAAP (More Advanced Individuals with Autism, Asperger Syndrome, and Pervasive Developmental Disorder). The two organizations have created a single resource for families, individuals, and medical professionals who deal with the challenges of Asperger syndrome, autism, and pervasive developmental disorder not otherwise specified. Their website provides articles; educational resources; links to local, national, and international support groups; sources of professional help; lists of camps and schools; conference information; recommended reading; and moderated support message boards.

Organization for Autism Research (OAR)
2000 N. Fourteenth St., Ste. 710
Arlington, VA 22201
(703) 243-9710
website: www
.researchautism.org

OAR is an organization that uses applied science to answer questions that parents, families, individuals with autism, teachers, and caregivers confront daily. OAR funds research on treatment, education, and statistics and publishes the *OARacle* newsletter, which can be found on its website. Entering the search term "Asperger" in the website search field yields hundreds of results.

Wrong Planet
2009 Bobwhite Ct.
Charlottesville, VA
22901
(213) 784-8615
e-mail: alex@wrong
planet.net
website: www.wrong
planet.net

Wrong Planet is an online community designed for individuals with Asperger syndrome, autism, attention-deficit/hyperactivity disorder, pervasive developmental disorders, and other neurological differences, as well as for family members and professionals concerned with these issues. The organization hosts a discussion forum, an article section, blogs, and a chatroom for real-time communication with other members.

FOR FURTHER READING

Books
Thomas Armstrong, *Neurodiversity: Discovering the Extraordinary Gifts of Autism, ADHD, Dyslexia, and Other Brain Differences.* Cambridge, MA: Da Capo Lifelong, 2010.

Tony Attwood, *The Complete Guide to Asperger's Syndrome.* London: Jessica Kingsley, 2007.

Tony Attwood et al. *Asperger's and Girls.* Arlington, VA: Future Horizons, 2006.

Michael John Carley, *Asperger's from the Inside Out.* Chicago: Perigee Trade, 2008.

Zachary Chastain and Phyllis Livingston, *A Different Drummer: Youth with Asperger's Syndrome.* Broomall, PA: Mason Crest, 2008.

Julie Clark, *Asperger's in Pink: A Guidebook for Raising (and Being!) a Girl with Asperger's Syndrome.* Arlington, VA: Future Horizons, 2010.

Judy Converse, *Special-Needs Kids Eat Right: Strategies to Help Kids on the Autism Spectrum Focus, Learn, and Thrive.* New York: Perigee, 2009.

Temple Grandin, *The Way I See It: A Personal Look at Autism and Asperger's.* Arlington, VA: Future Horizons, 2008.

Jeffrey E. Jessum, *Diary of a Social Detective: Real-Life Tales of Mystery, Intrigue and Interpersonal Adventure.* Shawnee Mission, KS: AAPC, 2011.

Lynn Kern Koegel and Claire LaZebnik, *Growing Up on the Spectrum: A Guide to Life, Love, and Learning for Teens and Young Adults with Autism and Asperger's.* New York: Viking Adult, 2009.

J.D. Kraus, *The Aspie Teen's Survival Guide: Candid Advice for Teens, Tweens, and Parents, from a Young Man with Asperger's Syndrome.* Arlington, VA: Future Horizons, 2010.

Jerry Newport, Mary Newport, and Johnny Dodd, *Mozart and the Whale: An Asperger's Love Story*. New York: Touchstone, 2007.

Paul A. Offit, *Autism's False Prophets: Bad Science, Risky Medicine, and the Search for a Cure*. New York: Columbia University Press, 2008.

Nancy J. Patrick, *Social Skills for Teenagers and Adults with Asperger Syndrome*. London: Jessica Kingsley, 2008.

Edward Ross Ritvo, *Understanding the Nature of Autism and Asperger's Disorder: Forty Years of Clinical Practice and Pioneering Research*. London: Jessica Kingsley, 2006.

Ron Rubio, *Mind/Body Techniques for Asperger's Syndrome: The Way of the Pathfinder*. London: Jessica Kingsley, 2008.

Clare Sainsbury, *Martian in the Playground: Understanding the Schoolchild with Asperger's Syndrome*. Rev. ed. Los Angeles: Sage, 2009.

Rudy Simone, *Asperger's on the Job: Must-Have Advice for People with Asperger's or High-Functioning Autism and their Employers, Educators, and Advocates*. Arlington, VA: Future Horizons, 2010.

Daniel Tammett, *Born on a Blue Day: Inside the Extraordinary Mind of an Autistic Savant*. New York: Free Press, 2007.

Periodicals and Internet Sources

Neil Amdur, "Asperger's Syndrome, On Screen and in Life," *New York Times*, August 4, 2009.

Jody Becker, "Behind the Autism Statistics," *Atlantic*, October 2009. www.theatlantic.com/magazine/archive/2009/10/behind-the-autism-statistics/7729.

Rebecca Berg, "Autism—an Environmental Health Issue After All?," *Journal of Environmental Health*, June 1, 2009.

Lori Berkowitz, "Perspectives of Autism from My Family," *LoriB.me*, April 25, 2010. http://lbnuke.com/2010/04/25/perspectives-of-autism-from-my-family.

Brian Bethune, "Autistic Licence: For Years, There Was Only 'Rain Man.' Suddenly, Asperger's Is the New 'It' Disorder On Screen and in Fiction," *Maclean's*, July 20, 2009.

Charlotte Brownlow and Lindsay O'Dell, "Representations of Autism: Implications for Community Healthcare Practice," *Community Practitioner*, July 2009.

Laura Burdon, "Asperger Syndrome and Offending Behaviour," *Learning Disability Practice*, November 2009.

Alicia Chang, "Autistic Teens Master Social Cues, Find Friends," PhysOrg, August 21, 2009. www.physorg.com/news170053709.html.

George Dvorsky, "Aspergers as Gift," Institute for Ethics & Emerging Technologies, November 27, 2008. http://ieet.org/index.php/IEET/more/dvorsky20081127.

David Finch, "Somewhere Inside, a Path to Empathy," *New York Times*, May 17, 2009.

Carlin Flora, "The Kiriana Conundrum," *Psychology Today*, November/December 2006.

Jesse Green, "The Leap," *New York*, June 7, 2010. http://nymag.com/news/features/66285.

Steven Higgs, "Simplifying the Definition of Autism: After 16 Years Asperger's Apparently Doesn't Exist," *Age of Autism*, June 8, 2010. www.ageofautism.com/2010/06/simplifying-the-definition-of-autism-after-16-years-aspergers-apparently-doesnt-exist.html.

Valerie Hobbs, "Imagine This (a Narrative on Bullying)," *Odd One Out*, February 12, 2008. http://lastcrazyhorn.wordpress.com/2008/02/12/imagine-this-a-narrative-on-bullying.

Mark Hyman, "Why Current Thinking About Autism Is Completely Wrong," *Huffington Post*, September 5, 2009. www.huffingtonpost.com/dr-mark-hyman/why-current-thinking-abou_b_275753.html.

Claudia Kalb, "Erasing Autism," *Newsweek*, May 25, 2009.

Scott Barry Kaufman, "Numbers Guy," *Psychology Today*, November/December 2009.

David Kirby, "EPA Study: Autism Boom Began in 1988, Environmental Factors Are Assumed," *Huffington Post*, April 23, 2010. www.huffingtonpost.com/david-kirby/autism-vaccine-epa-study_b_548837.html.

Tracy Mayor, "IT's Open Secret: Asperger's Syndrome Has Been a Part of IT for as Long as IT Has Existed. So Why Aren't We Talking About It?," *Computerworld*, May 5, 2008.

Deborah Orr, "Simon Baron-Cohen: Ali G's Smarter Cousin and Britain's Leading Expert on Autism," *Independent* (London), May 23, 2009.

Catherine Quinn, "Genetics Research Suggests Links Between Common Disorders," *Learning Disability Practice*, November 2009.

Cynthia Ramnarace, "Your Best Shot," *Kiwi*, July/August 2008. www.kiwimagonline.com/articles/articlepage.php?art_id=120&cat_id=4&full=l.

Joseph Shapiro, "Autism Movement Seeks Acceptance, Not Cures," NPR, June 26, 2006. www.npr.org/templates/story/story.php?storyId=5488463.

Lynne Soraya, "Asperger Emotions and Adult Relationships," *Psychology Today*, September 7, 2008. www.psychologytoday.com/node/1740.

———, "It's Different for Girls: Is Diagnosis by Brain Scan Ready for Prime Time?," *Psychology Today*, August 12, 2010. www.psychologytoday.com/blog/aspergers-diary/201008/its-different-girls.

Maia Szalavitz, "Asperger's Theory Does About-Face; Rather than Ignoring Others, Researchers Think Spectrum Sufferers Care Too Much," *Toronto (ON) Star*, May 14, 2009.

Sherri Tenpenny, "Vaccines: Veterinarians Are Better than Human Doctors," *Huffington Post*, April 16, 2010. www.huffingtonpost.com/dr-sherri-tenpenny/vaccines-veterinarians-ar_b_533505.html.

Louise Tickle, "Employing Adults with Autism: Don't Write Them Off," *Guardian* (Manchester, UK), October 17, 2009. www.guardian.co.uk/money/2009/oct/17/employing-adults-with-autism.

Janet Treasure, "Is Anorexia the Female Asperger's?," *Times* (London), August 17, 2007.

Claudia Wallis, "A Powerful Identity, a Vanishing Diagnosis," *New York Times*, November 3, 2009.

INDEX